Fungi for Gardeners

DK

Fungi for Gardeners

Know Your Garden Fungi and How to Grow Them

Dr. Jassy Drakulic

Contents

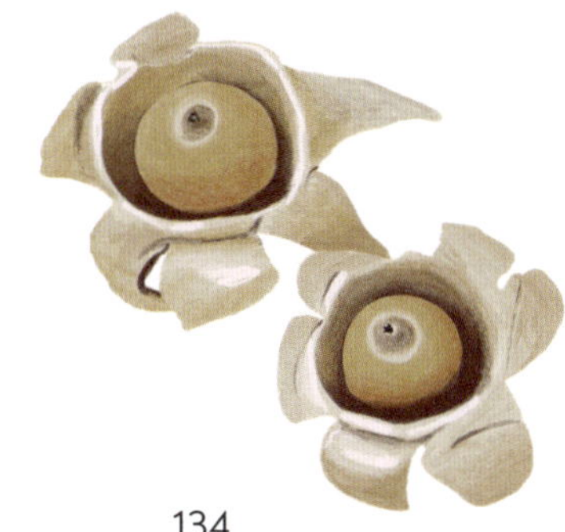

Disclaimer

Many fungi are poisonous and can cause serious harm or death on contact or consumption. Collection is at the reader's own risk. The information in this book is not comprehensive and should not be relied upon for accurate identification or for any medical or diagnostic purpose. Just because a fungus is not mentioned as being poisonous does not mean that it is safe to consume. The authors and publishers disclaim, as far as the law allows, any liability arising directly or indirectly from the use or misuse of the information contained in this book.

THE FUNGI MANIFESTO

Have you noticed that there is a fungi revolution happening? Previously underappreciated, kingdom Fungi is now popping up in the press, in novel products on supermarket shelves, and even in movies and TV. But knowing how this all translates to your own patch of earth can be mystifying for many gardeners. This book explains how fungi work and how to help them thrive in your garden. Fungi are not just another trend; they precede plants in evolutionary history and have been paving the way for plants to flourish ever since.

Through my work answering fungi inquiries for the RHS Gardening Advice service, I know that many gardeners are suspicious of fungi because of how harmful pathogenic fungi can be. Ask a gardener to name a fungus and honey fungus usually comes up first. This is understandable, as honey fungus is hugely prevalent and can have serious impacts on the look and function of a garden.

Fungi are much more widely studied for their harm than their good, but gardeners can gain a lot by shaking off this preoccupation with disease. Healthier gardens await those who welcome and appreciate the abundance of beneficial fungi.

My own entry into fungal science (mycology) came through plant pathology. Since joining the RHS in 2016, I have researched honey fungus and its root rot, seeking to understand its biology in gardens and developing affordable and sustainable ways to minimize its damage. Through this endeavor, I realized that gardeners can get

Fungi are already at work doing good in your garden and you can get more out of them by understanding what they do and what they need to thrive.

better results and value for money by working with nature rather than by trying to control it. I was also won over by the magnificence and beauty of mushrooms and fungal forms.

In recent years, I have devoted more of my time to learning how to notice and identify wild fungi and understanding the ways fungi interact with each other, plants, and the environment. I have spent several years researching, experimenting, and communing with scientists and growers so I could create advice, resources, and learning opportunities for gardeners about fungi that reflect the frontiers of scientific evidence and understanding, which have shaped the contents of this book.

The wide range of roles performed by fungi are covered here, from recyclers to mycorrhizae and a few of the key large-fruiting pathogens. Walking through the different habitats within a garden, I will introduce you to a selection of the most common and widespread species to spot.

Contributors from across the UK and Europe have helped me develop native outdoor fungal cultivation projects at RHS Wisley. I'll show you how to use the same methods in cultivation projects at home so that you can experiment with growing fungi, either for fresh, healthy food, or for their medicinal or wildlife benefits.

Fungi provide the foundations for all other life in the garden to flourish.

Fruiting bodies are wonderful, but the hidden mycelia in gardens are owed the greatest celebration. Here are some of the biggest reasons to celebrate and support the fungi in your garden.

Fungi create healthy soils
By releasing nutrients from dead plant material, fungi improve the health of soils. Wood is a formidable composition of waterproofed and reinforced polymers, but the fungi that have evolved side by side with woody plants have developed a remarkable biological toolkit to dismantle and recycle it. The white rot fungi break down lignin into biologically available organic matter that makes soils nutritious and water retentive. The brown rot fungi leave behind an altered form of lignin, creating a porous material that shelters invertebrates and microbes. As decaying matter falls to the ground, soil-borne fungi continue its decomposition. Their long, winding cells weave between and bind soil particles, improving its structure and nutritional quality. Fungal mycelium also acts as a carbon store.

Fungi support water management
By decaying dead material, fungi generate spongy wood and rotting leaf litter that absorbs heavy rainfall, which slowly releases water back into soils as it dries. Covering bare soil with fungi and their foodstuffs stabilizes the soil's temperature and prevents it from drying out in hot weather. Fungi growing in and on plants help them tolerate drought or waterlogging.

Fungi support plant health and create healthy ecosystems
Mycorrhizal fungi partner closely with plant roots. Few plants can thrive without them, relying on the enhanced provisions of nutrients and water that fungi make available. Fungi live quietly on and in all plants, above and below ground, helping them defend themselves more effectively against pathogen attacks. Richer communities of fungi in soil limit the potency and movement of pathogens. Fungi provide food and create habitats for wildlife. They drive garden ecosystems to become resilient and self-regulating, rich in diverse species spanning the

kingdoms of life, from bacteria to bees and bats.

Fungi do more good than harm
Even while the total number of named fungi is biased toward those that harm plants, only 5 percent are pathogens. Most of those cause isolated damage and few can kill plants. The proportion of mushroom-forming fungi that are pathogens is even smaller, a main concern as there may be other pathogens that are more worrisome in a particular area. Most mushrooms appearing in gardens are usually signs that fungi are supporting the plants there, by helping to build better soils. Likewise, for the fungi in and on leaves, roots, and stems, for every harmful example, there are many more species doing something helpful. Instead of trying to control those that do harm, we could be encouraging the fungi that bring balance and stability.

Habitat fragmentation threatens kingdom Fungi
Fungi support ecosystems all over the world, yet thousands, if not millions, of fungal species are at risk of extinction due to pollution, climate change, and particularly because their natural habitats are being destroyed. Gardens cannot replace long-lived woodlands and forests that are the most valued sites for fungal conservation, but if all those who garden come to respect and cherish fungi, maybe our leaders and communities will do more to protect these unseen life forms that underpin our very existence.

All gardens can be fungi gardens
Overall, this book aims to explain what fungi are, what they do, and how to work with them to get the best from your garden. What fits in these pages is just a starting point; at the back, you will find my recommendations to take your learning further. I hope that after gaining this understanding, you will be convinced that fungi belong in gardens and are inspired to nurture a rich community of fungi in yours.

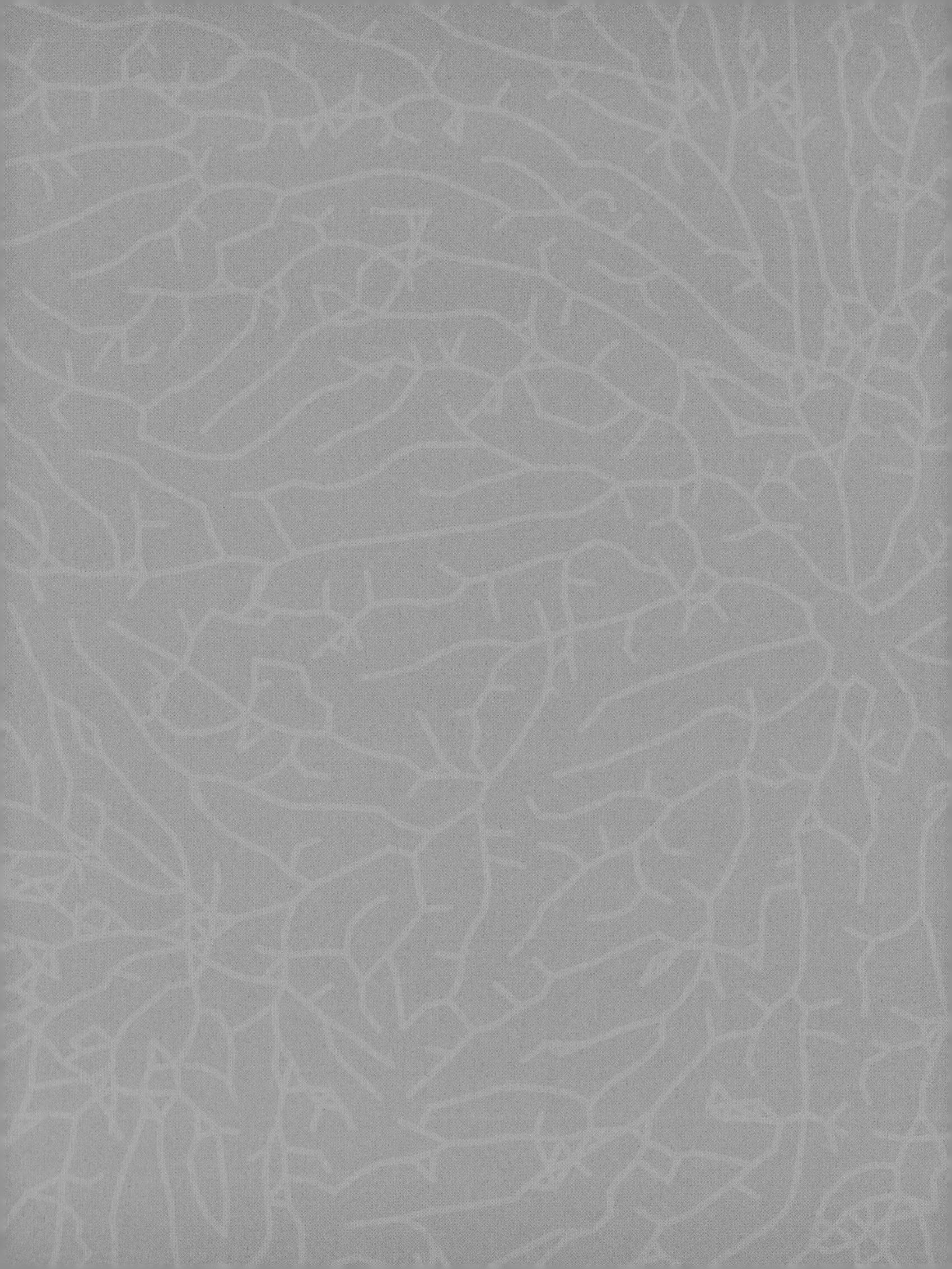

Know your fungi

WHAT ARE FUNGI?

Fungi largely exist out of sight, often growing as microscopic, threadlike cells called hyphae. A connected network of these cells creates the bulk of the fungus, the mycelium.

As hyphae grow longer, elongating at the tips, the mycelium gets larger. Fungi grow vegetatively like this to search and compete for food, space, and water, comparable to a plant forming new shoots. If food runs out, mycelium can shrink by withdrawing the contents of unfed hyphae and using the reclaimed resources to grow elsewhere.

Visible or invisible?

Usually, all we can see of fungi are their fruiting bodies—reproductive structures built from hyphae to release spores, comparable to flowers and pollen. Fungi are hugely diverse, spanning upward of two million species; this book focuses on two subgroups and their fruiting bodies: the basidiomycota (spore droppers), and the ascomycota (spore shooters). Other fungi may not make mycelia or spores, or instead make microscopic fruiting bodies or have multiple spore types.

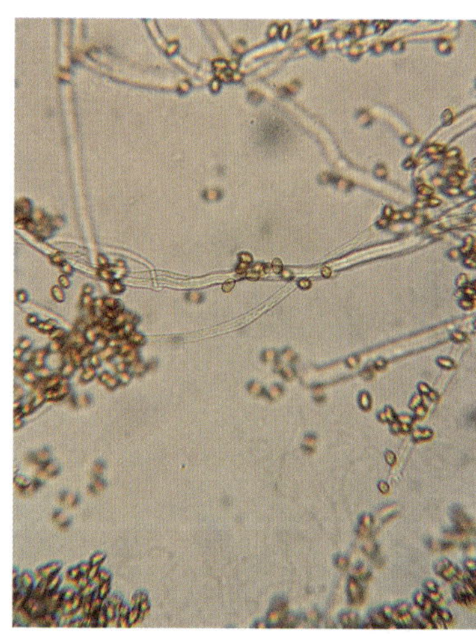

OPPOSITE BELOW LEFT Mycelium of these fairy inkcaps (*Coprinellus disseminatus*) is hidden inside the log they are growing on.

OPPOSITE BELOW RIGHT Microscopic spores and hyphae.

LEFT Many connected hyphae form a mycelium.

Food for fungi

Unlike plants, fungi need food from the environment to survive. Unlike animals, fungi cannot pick up their food, chew it, and digest it internally. Instead, fungi grow toward their food and absorb it. For complex food sources, they grow toward and throughout it, exuding enzymes to break it down into sugars, amino acids, and fats, and absorbing what they need.

Roles of beneficial fungi

Recycler fungi, known as saprotrophs, digest and decay dead material for their food. They create soils by decomposing organic debris, releasing the nutrition that had been locked away within it so it can be used as the building blocks for new living cells.

Fungi are also a key component in the microbiomes of garden plants. For every flower, leaf, and root that you see, there will be countless fungal hyphae there as well. The fungi that form highly specialized partnerships with plant roots are known as mycorrhizae, while others that live discreetly anywhere inside plants are called endophytes. Both types gain their nutrition from excess sugars the plant makes.

For most of its life, a fungus grows out of sight underground, growing vegetatively as a mass of threadlike cells called mycelium.

LIFE CYCLE

Many fungi reproduce and spread farther afield by making spores from a fruiting body. It is usually this part that is visible to humans and includes the structures we call mushrooms or toadstools.

Kingdom or queendom?

Spores can be compared to plant pollen because both are microscopic "sex cells" that must fertilize another sex cell to form a new individual. However, unlike pollen and ova, spores are neither male nor female and can be one of many mating types. With its defiance of binary sexual labels, kingdom Fungi is often alternatively referred to as a queendom.

To start the process, the vegetative mycelium grows into a new, complex form that develops spores, protects them as they mature, and then helps their release into the environment. We call these forms fruiting bodies (see pp16–21) and they make billions of spores. Many spores fall close to the fruiting body, but millions make it up into air currents and move long distances on the wind. Spores eventually fall from the air on raindrops while those that never make it into the air may get dragged around on the bodies of mobile creatures (humans included).

If a spore lands somewhere with food and the right environmental cues, it germinates into an infertile mycelium. It then needs to survive long enough to grow into contact with another spore-borne mycelium that has a suitable mating type.

If the spores' mycelia can successfully fuse together, they form one fertile individual, which may go on to make fruiting bodies of its own. Each spore has different genetic traits—those that are suited to the environments they land in are more likely to survive and go on to reproduce, meaning their advantageous traits become more frequent with each generation.

Creating huge numbers of spores helps fungi compete with each other and adapt to new environments.

Release of spores
Spores are released and are usually carried on the wind.

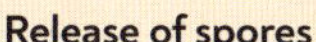

Fruiting body grows
A fertile mycelium produces a fruiting body to spread its spores.

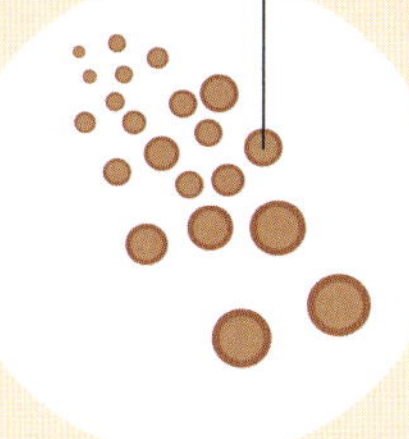

CREATING NEW INDIVIDUALS

Spores get dealt a unique combination of their parents' genes, and new, fertile mycelia formed after spore germination of fusion (mating) have traits from both parents.

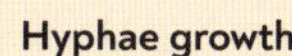

Hyphae growth
The spores land, germinate into hyphae, and create an infertile mycelium.

Mating types
Instead of sexes, fungi have mating types, and some species have thousands of combinations.

Fusion of hyphae
The hyphae from the mycelia of two compatible spore types join together, forming a new, fertile mycelium.

FRUITING BODIES

Fruiting bodies are structures that fungi create and release spores from. Some will form and fade within hours; others endure for years. The general types of forms can be categorized based on their overall shape and where the spores are produced, but fungi with the same fruiting body types can come from entirely different families, and four types of greatest relevance to gardeners are as follows.

Mushrooms
Mushrooms, alternatively called toadstools, are the most recognizable fruiting bodies. They consist of a round cap supported on a stalk. They are typical of spore-dropping fungi (the Basidiomycota division of the kingdom Fungi), where spores form on the outside of tissues under the cap such as gills, pores, or spines, then drop away freely when mature.

Cups
The typical fruiting body forms for the spore shooters (the Ascomycota) are shallow, bowl-like cups. Embedded within the inner surface are spores, held in long, oval chambers, waiting to be shot out quickly.

Polypores
Polypores grow horizontally out of wood and so are commonly referred to as brackets. They drop spores from pores (the openings of many tiny tubes arranged side by side) positioned underneath the fruiting body. They can be annuals that last a few months and are grown anew each year or perennials that slowly enlarge as the years go by.

Stomach fungi
These fruiting bodies, also known as sac fungi, comprise a protective sac filled with microscopic spores. Once mature, a hole opens in the top, and when raindrops or animals (such as a playful human) nudge them, spores billow outward.

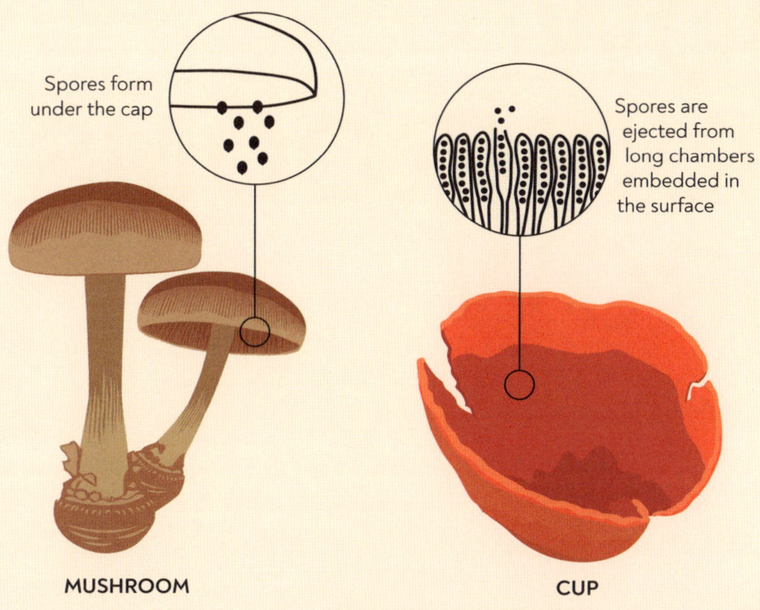
Spores form
under the cap
Spores are
ejected from
long chambers
embedded in
the surface
MUSHROOM
CUP

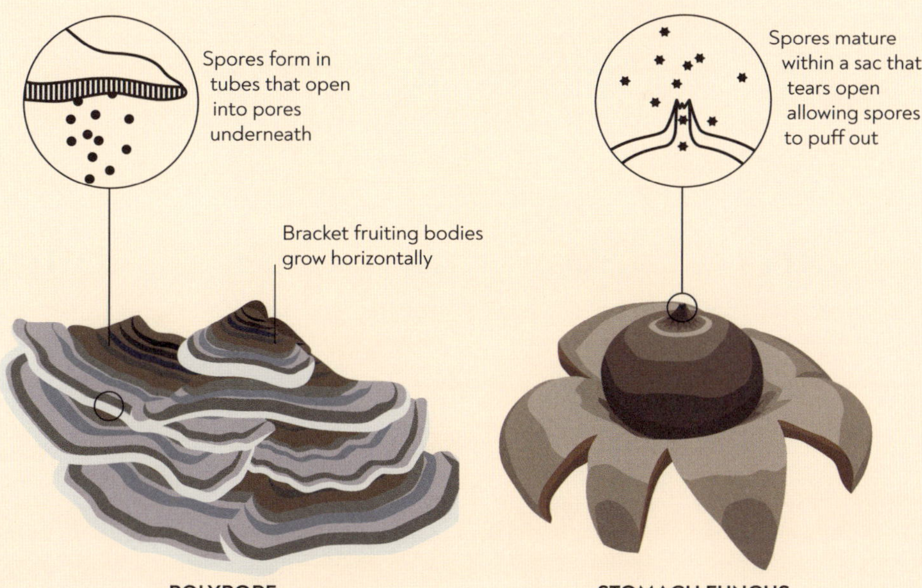
Spores form in
tubes that open
into pores
underneath
Bracket fruiting bodies
grow horizontally
Spores mature
within a sac that
tears open
allowing spores
to puff out
POLYPORE
STOMACH FUNGUS

HOW MUSHROOMS GROW

Mushrooms may seem familiar, but the closer you look, the more complex they appear.

Early growth

The first stage of mushroom formation is a dense knot of mycelium. This swells and differentiates into a compact version of a mushroom contained within a sac called the universal veil. The stem then extends upward, tearing open the veil tissue as it elongates. Remnants of the veil may remain around the stem base or stick to the cap, as with white spots on the fly agaric (*Amanita muscaria*). The cap begins closed and joined to the stem by another veil of tissue, the partial veil, which keeps the spores protected as they develop within the spore-carrying layer. As the stem reaches its full

Rapid change

Knowing mushrooms' growth phases helps make sense of how well developed any specimens are.

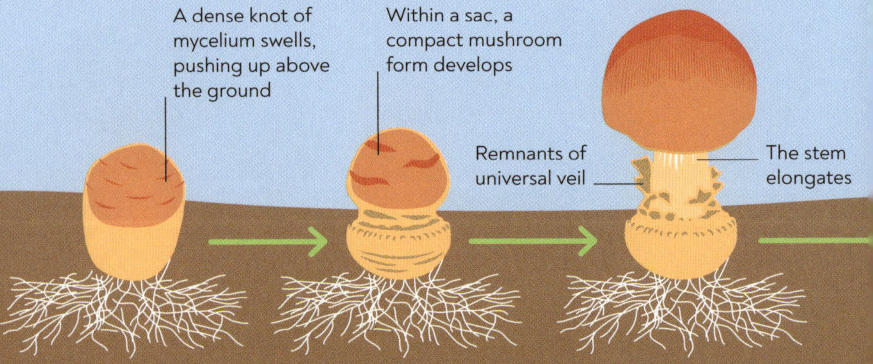

A dense knot of mycelium swells, pushing up above the ground

Within a sac, a compact mushroom form develops

Remnants of universal veil

The stem elongates

height, the cap opens outward, with different species opening into a dome, a flat disc, or inverting into a goblet shape. Remnants of the partial veil that held the immature cap closed may be left on the stem as a ring. This could be faint traces of mycelium, a draping skirt, or wisps stuck to the cap edges, often stained with the color of the spores.

Spore release and reproduction
Spores mature underneath the caps and are released into humid air spaces lining gills, pore tubes, or spines. Gravity, air currents, rain, and wildlife can all help spread spores farther afield. Once the mushroom has shed most of its spores, the cap and stem will wither and decay.

GILL SPACING

The way the gills are arranged can help with species identification.

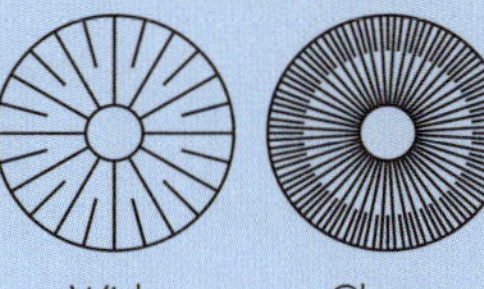

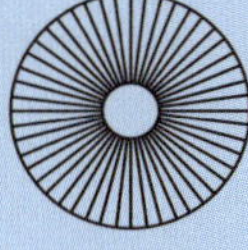
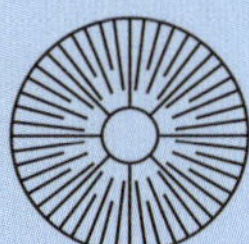

GILL ATTACHMENT

Look for the different ways gills attach to the stem.

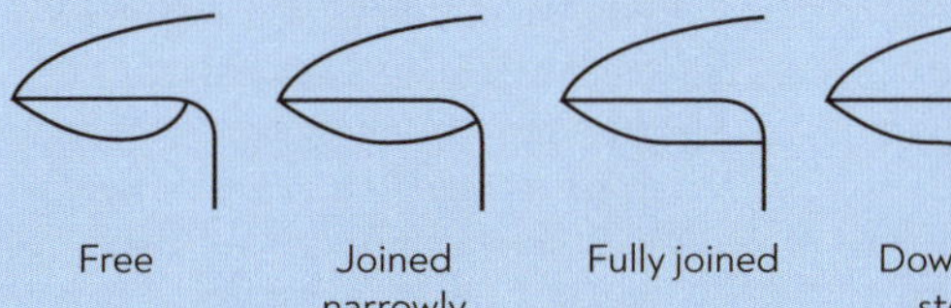

The cap expands and breaks the partial veil

Remnants of the partial veil

Ring

The cap opens fully and mature spores fall from the underside

THE BEAUTY OF FRUITING BODIES

Fungal fruiting bodies add an extra layer of beauty and intrigue to gardens. Their fleeting nature makes them exhilarating to stumble across, with colors ranging from pastels to saturated hues, in flat matte to mirror-gloss finishes. Many little brown mushrooms exist, but showier species have striking colors like yellow stagshorn (*Calocera viscosa*), blue roundhead (*Stropharia caerulea*), and amethyst deceiver (*Laccaria amethystina*). Several will change color when bruised or after rain.

Shapes and details

Fruiting bodies contribute novel shapes in assorted sizes, from bulky constructions that suddenly materialize to intricate miniature specimens that would be fitting as dollhouse accessories.

Looking closely reveals a range of embellishments like hairs, scales, warts, pleats, or crystals. The spore-bearing layer has its own visual treats, from the precise pointillism of pores to mesmerizing irises of gills, gaping widely or packed as tightly as the pages of a book.

Scents and textures

Many fungi provide attractive scents and textures. Most are pleasantly cool to the touch, but some are sticky or strokable, like velvet shank (*Flammulina velutipes*) caps and stems. Foul-smelling stinkhorns (*Phallus impudicus*, see p77) are notorious, but others, like perfumed blewits (*Collybia nuda* formerly *Lepista*) and radish-scented bonnets (*Mycena* spp.), have unexpected and appealing aromas.

Fungi offer a wealth of sensory experience, ranging in color, texture, and scent.

TOP LEFT Yellow stagshorn (*Calocera viscosa*).

ABOVE Blue roundhead (*Stropharia caerulea*).

CENTRE LEFT Amethyst deceiver (*Laccaria amethystina*) gills.

LEFT Yellow fairy cups (*Bisporella citrina*).

FUNGI IN THE ECOSYSTEM

Fungi transform gardens into thriving ecosystems by creating networks that support beneficial species.

Decay drives diversity
Fungi initiate the breakdown of complex plant polymers like lignin and cellulose. No other life-form is able to do this. Fungi secrete powerful enzymes that transform those polymers into simpler molecules, including sugars. Some are absorbed to feed the fungus, but much is left behind. The remnants of the dead material are softened and inviting to other organisms that can continue the breakdown process. Within old trees, fungi excavate the inner dead heartwood and form hollows that often become nesting sites for birds, bats, and pollinators. Fungi also convert piles of woodchip into humus—a spongy layer that mulches the soil, protecting and nourishing the wildlife within it.

The presence of fungi in soil and their decomposition of organic matter creates new habitats and unlocks sustenance. This attracts and supports a wealth of biodiversity, particularly invertebrates, including pollinators, natural enemies of herbivores, and later-stage decomposers (such as springtails and slugs). Likewise, fungal activity attracts other microbes that aid decomposition, improve nutrient cycling, and can convert nitrogen gas into a form plants can use.

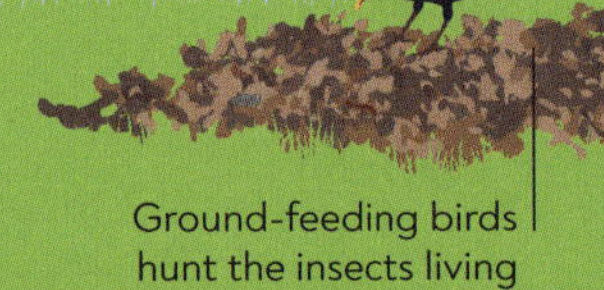

Ground-feeding birds hunt the insects living in fruiting bodies

Fungal fruiting bodies and decomposing material are havens for wildlife, providing habitats and sources of food.

Fruiting bodies support wildlife

Fungal fruiting bodies provide food and shelter and can be a hunting ground for animals and microbes. Flies and beetles lay their eggs in fruiting bodies, and when they hatch, the larvae feed on the fungal flesh. Fruiting bodies and spores are an important source of nutrition and vitamins for wildlife. Even out of fruiting season, mycelium and lichens are the grazing stock for all sorts of fungivorous life.

A biodiverse garden

Having lots of fungi in gardens encourages more wildlife and microbes to make their homes there too.

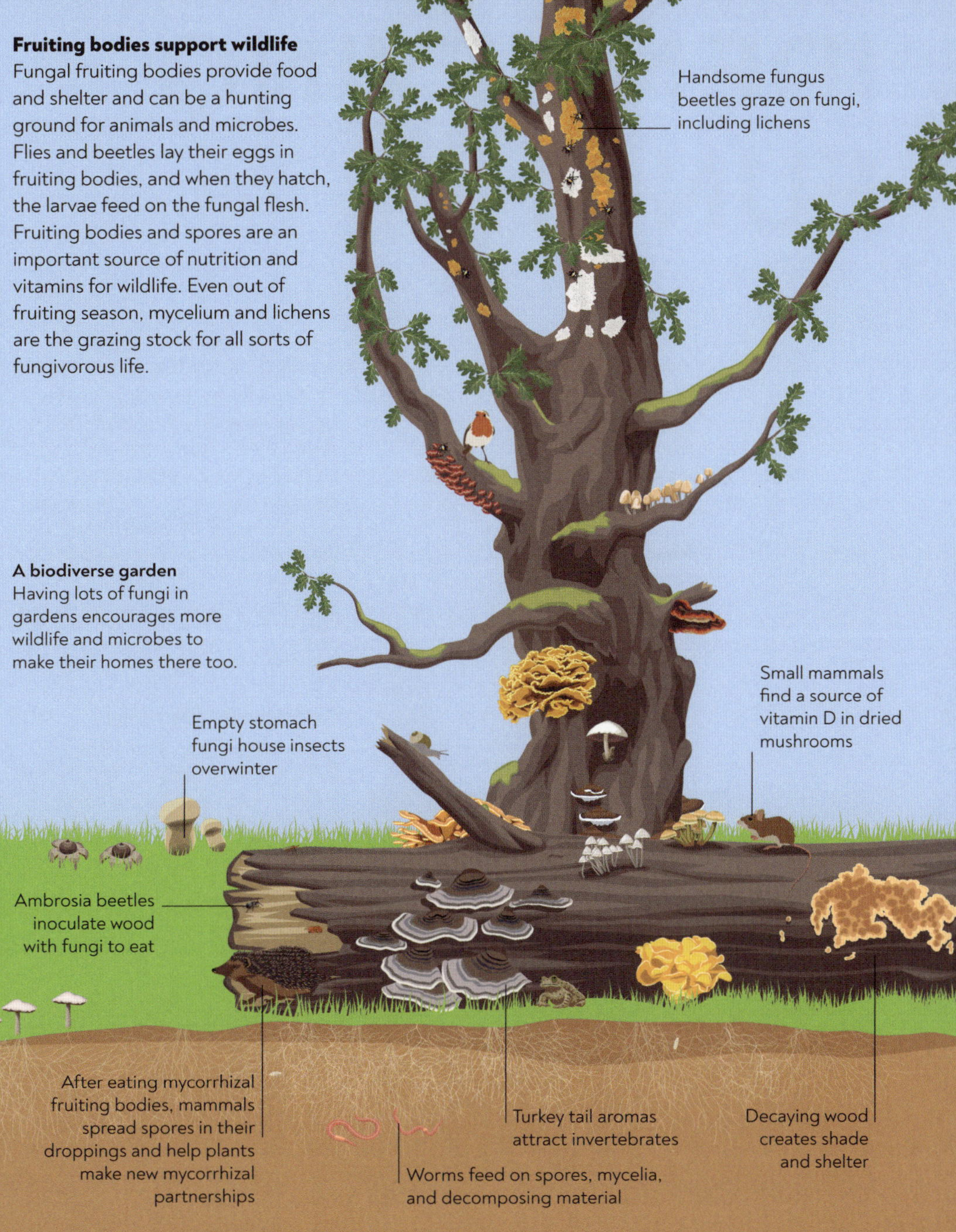

IDENTIFYING FUNGI

Identifying fruiting bodies involves building a profile of their growth form and habitat. Some tools that can help include a penknife, ruler, hand lens, collecting box, notebook and pencil, camera, and a flat piece of glassware.

Where to start

Begin by looking at the habitat, the host plants, substrate, or soil type where the fungi are fruiting. Get a clear view by brushing away leaves or grass and take close-up photographs showing the top, sides, and underneath, including an object for scale, like a ruler or coin. Pick up the fruiting body to observe and smell it while it is fresh, as these attributes can change over time. Use a hand lens to help notice all its textures and colors. For mushrooms, cut around the stem base with your knife to view its entire length. Cut a cross section to see the internal structure and observe if the flesh changes color or oozes liquid. Take measurements and annotate photos or a sketch to help you keep track of your observations.

Determine the spore color

You may be able to see spore color, but often you'll need to make a spore print to see this. Cut a section of the fruiting body that will fit on top of a flat, clear backdrop like a glass plate or microscope slide and place it spore-side down. If you don't have flat glass on hand, foil or black and white paper work. Cover with a plastic box or a bowl, and leave

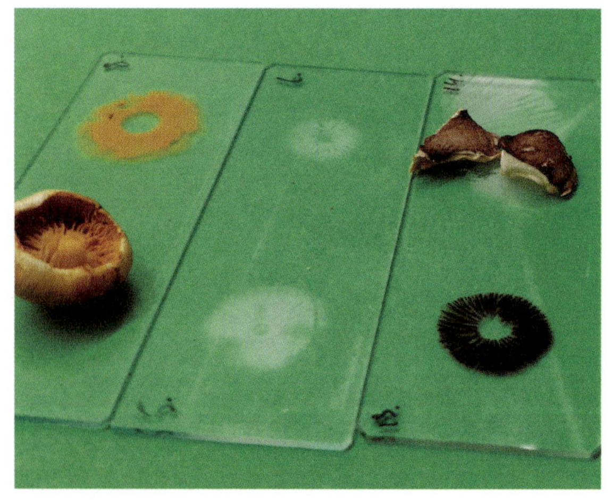

Spore printing
If you don't have glassware, you can make a spore print on crockery, foil, or paper instead.

for at least two hours. Remove the box and lift up the fruiting body segment. If you can't see the spore color, then add a drop of water on top and leave it a while longer before revealing.

Finding a name

Use the profile you've created to figure out which group your fungus belongs to by following a key or comparing against fungi wheels (see p139). Compare your specimen's profile to photos and descriptions for species of that group in guide books.

Some species are unmistakable, but others have subtle or transient differences. You may not know what to look for without prior experience, but you will learn faster with the help of others in local fungi groups or online communities.

Further investigation

Despite your best efforts, some species are impossible to distinguish without the use of a microscope to check the spores or cellular features. Enthusiasts can invest in high-end equipment, but you can get a lot done with a relatively low-cost student compound microscope and an eyepiece measuring device or USB camera for taking spore measurements. Even then, tricky fungal groups need DNA fingerprinting to distinguish their members, and a growing number of fungal recording enthusiasts have a setup to do this from home.

It takes time to learn how to identify fungi. Expect to make mistakes, but do not permit yourself mistakes when identifying fungi to eat.

IDENTIFICATION APPS

Some fruiting bodies can be recognized from visible features, and image recognition software may be capable of identifying these. Recognition will be most reliable for common and unmistakable species. You will develop better skills and understanding by trying to find your own answers.

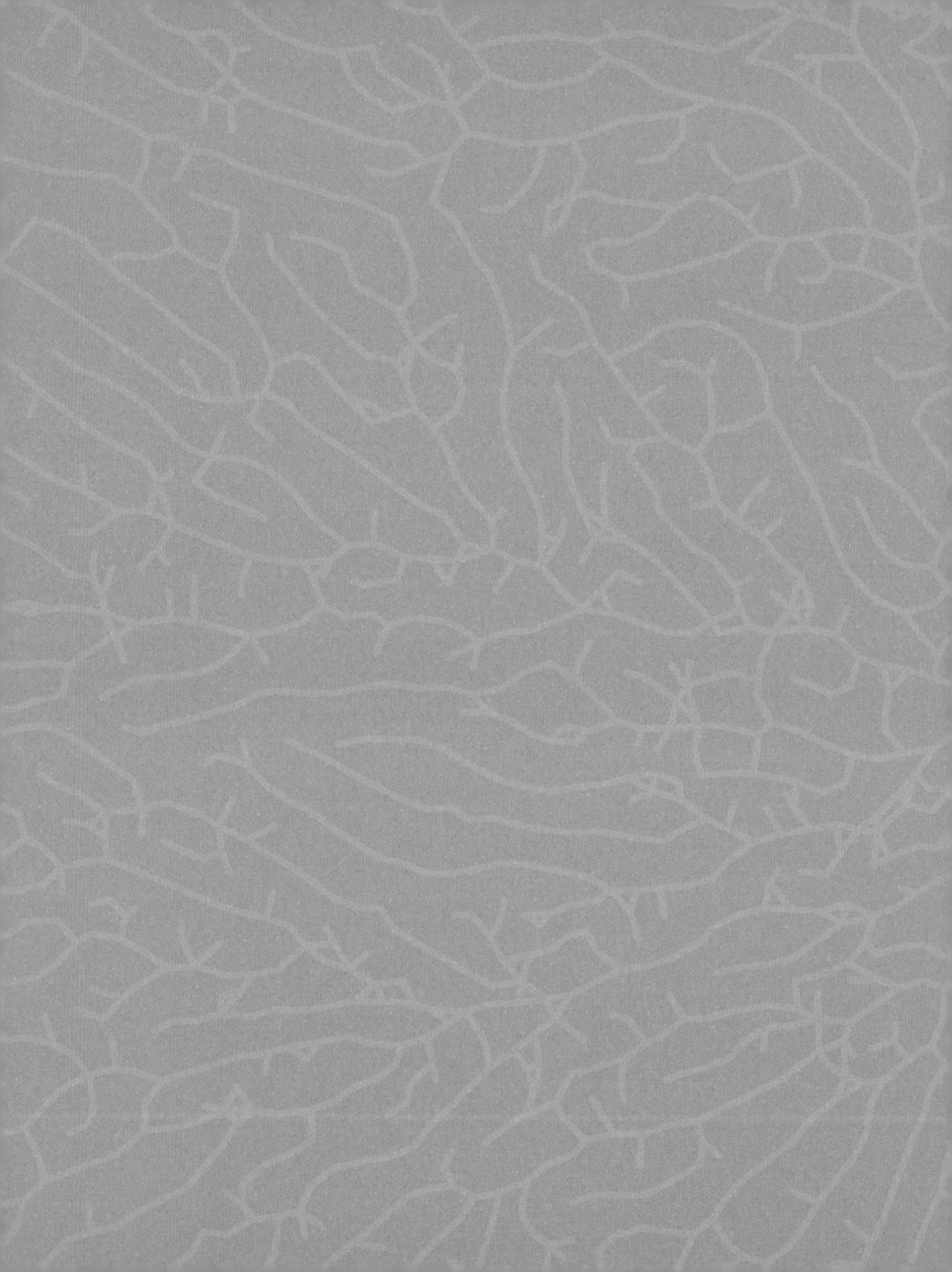

Fungi and where to find them

HABITAT

Fungi grow in many different habitats, from living trees to woodchip on garden paths. The fungi growing in and on plants play different roles ranging from supportive partners to subversive pathogens. Gardens contain unique combinations of plants and design features that encourage specific types of fungi. While the range of fungal species in gardens differs from that in natural landscapes, the roles fungi perform are universal, so understanding how fungi live and work in your garden explains how fungi underpin ecosystems around the world.

To help you get to know some of the fungi that support your garden ecosystem, this chapter explores the different habitats of a garden and describes the wild fungi that make visible fruiting bodies there. These pages cover select native species that are common in gardens.

Habitat conservation

At the time of writing, only a tiny fraction of known fungi have been assessed in accordance with methods accepted by the International Union for Conservation of Nature (IUCN), and most of these are in decline. Precious wild fungal habitats like old growth forests (that have developed undisturbed over a long period of time) are ever decreasing in area or becoming polluted. Replanting young trees does not replace old trees that took decades or centuries to peak in their ecological significance. To elevate fungi and wildlife biodiversity, it is crucial to protect trees through old age and after they die.

In some cases, gardens provide valued havens for vulnerable species, or they can help join up sites with higher importance for fungal conservation. Additionally, gardeners who gain familiarity with fungi in their plot can lend their support to efforts for conserving wild fungi.

Native versus nonnative fungi

Fungi travel around the world through human trade and travel, often arriving unintentionally on timber, soil, or live plants. Nonnative fungi that establish in a new place may compete with native fungi and force changes in their fungal communities. While some do this without spreading elsewhere, like the redlead roundhead (*Leratiomyces ceres*), others become invasive, taking over habitats and causing decline in the variety of local fungi. One example of this is the cultivated golden oyster (*Pleurotus citrinopileatus*).

GOLDEN OYSTER

REDLEAD ROUNDHEAD

Golden oyster (*Pleurotus citrinopileatus*) escaped cultivation in the US and is spreading into wild habitats. Redlead roundhead (*Leratiomyces ceres*) was introduced to Europe from Australia on traded wood, but mostly occurs in man-made woodchip habitats.

LION'S MANE

CORAL TOOTH

Protective laws exist for only a few fungi in certain countries, like lion's mane, also known as bearded tooth (*Hericium erinaceus*) in the UK, while its close relative coral tooth (*H. coralloides*) is rarer yet unprotected.

FORAGING

Finding and eating wild-grown food is an immersive way to connect with nature. Foragers abide by a code of conduct to treat species and ecosystems with utmost respect. Whether foraging for fungi or plants, do your research and eat only species that you can identify with certainty. Sometimes a fungus might be edible, but the growing context might make it unsafe to eat, for instance, fungi on yew trees (which are toxic) or next to polluted roads.

Identify the species

The most reliable way to identify edible species is to be accompanied by an experienced forager. Then you can return to the same site where you know those fungi grow. To find edible fungi for yourself, select sites that match the habitat and host preferences for the species you are looking for and visit regularly. If you are not on public land, you need to check whether foraging is permitted. Never forage on sensitive sites (such as Sites of Special Scientific Interest).

Picking

If you pick fruiting bodies, it won't weaken the mycelium of a fungus. The structures will be eaten one way or another, by wildlife or microbes, if not by you. The difference is any fruiting bodies that you take away won't drop as many of their spores, so pick only common species that you can identify in the field. Twisting them away from their substrate keeps them fresher for longer than slicing them, because cut cells lose water and degrade faster.

Protecting fungi

Pick sparingly for personal use, leaving most of what you find to complete their life cycles, serve wildlife, and display their beauty to others. Heavy foot traffic around tree roots compacts soils, so stick to paths where possible. For a list of currently threatened fungi, go to the International Union for Conservation of Nature (IUCN) website at www.iucnredlist.org and use the North America filter.

OPPOSITE Some species like golden chanterelles (*Cantharellus cibarius*) and white hedgehog mushrooms (*Hydnum repandum*) are easier to identify in the field than others.

WOODCHIP

Woodchip looks attractive as garden pathways or mulch and provides many benefits to gardens. Certain recycler fungi thrive in this habitat, either arriving as spores or already present as endophytes inside the wood before it was chipped. Fungi that flourish in woodchip have to tolerate exposed conditions but are rewarded by an ample supply of wood to feed on and rot down.

Benefits to soil

Fungal decay of woodchips creates humus with excellent water and temperature regulation that attracts invertebrates and resists compaction.

Some gardeners are wary of laying woodchip down because they have been told that it will take nitrogen from the soil. Nitrogen levels at the surface can drop at first, but deeply buried roots are not harmed by this, and once the chip rots down, the soil will gain much more nitrogen overall.

Local is best

The closer to home you can source your wood, the better. Fungi that are already present in locally sourced healthy wood will be acclimatized and established in your area so will perform better. Signs that fungi are thriving in woodchip can include visible white mycelium bonding chips together or the formation of fruiting bodies. Mushrooms on woodchips often appear in large crowds that can really put on a show. However, you can easily miss the tiny fruiting bodies of those like bird's nest fungi (Nidulariaceae, see p37), which are worth looking closely for.

Fruiting bodies in woodchip can appear in large numbers and put on quite a show.

Woodchip paths resist compaction and soil erosion

White mycelium
might be visible
Versatile and valuable
Woodchips have several uses in gardens. Recycler fungi slowly degrade them to release nutrition for themselves, plants, and other wildlife.
To grow woodchip fungi, give each species its own space
Add fresh chips to keep fungi well fed
Lay mulch in a donut, avoiding tree trunks
Raised beds filled with woodchip and fungal spawn can be used to cultivate fruiting bodies

HARE'S FOOT INKCAP

Scientific name *Coprinopsis lagopus*

Distribution Widespread and common across most temperate zones

Habitat Woodchip or humus-rich soil

When to see Spring to late fall

Type Mushroom

Spore production Gills

Spores

These slender gray caps are covered with white "fur" and are thought to resemble hares' feet. They appear in crowds, pushed upward on translucent hollow stems covered with minute hairs. The cap opens out then inverts as the edges curl upward.

Spore production
Crowded gills, free from the stem, are white, quickly turning dark from spores. Spores are smooth ovals, narrower than other similar relatives (e.g., *C. lagopides*).

Sensory characteristics
They sometimes have an aromatic scent. The gills "deliquesce," meaning they digest themselves, so all that is left is a sticky, spore-filled liquid.

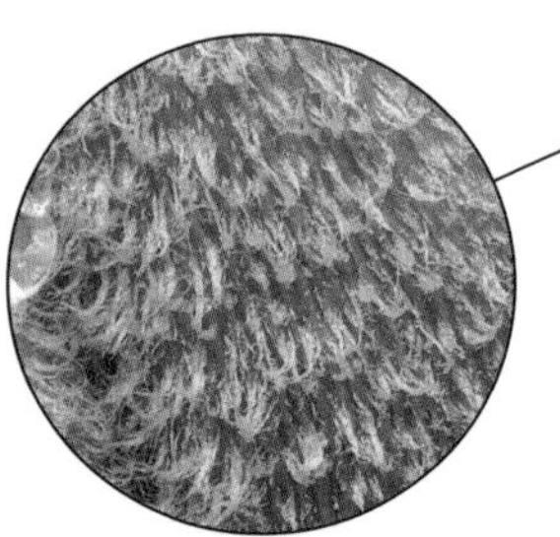

Furry white coating
Remnants of the universal veil cover young caps and stems but soon disappear.

Exquisitely beautiful, fragile, and fleeting mushrooms that appear and disappear again within a single day.

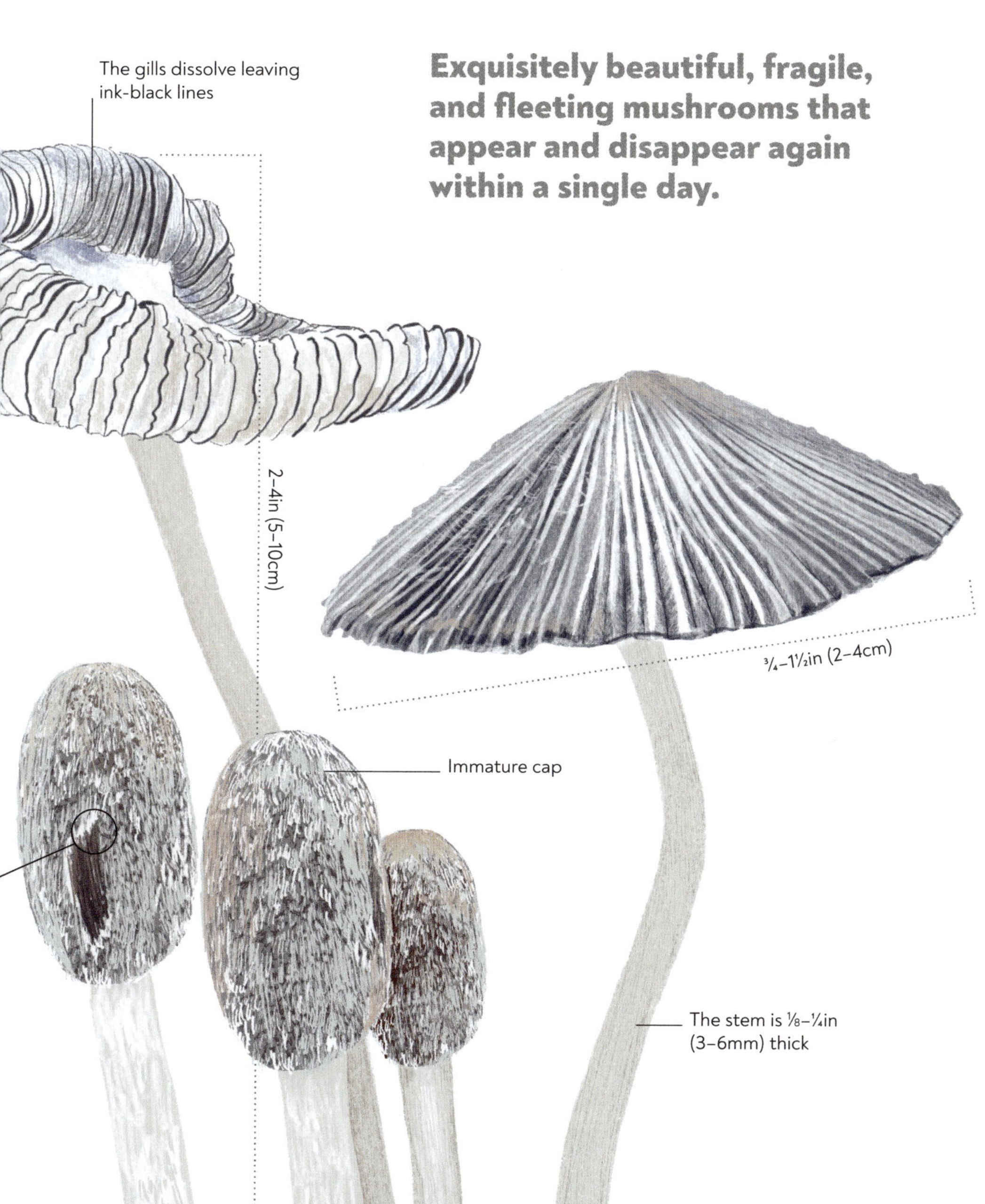

SCURFY TWIGLET

Scientific name
Tubaria furfuracea

Distribution Common and widespread worldwide

Habitat Woodchip, twigs, and other woody debris

When to see All year, peaking during mild winters

Type Mushroom

Spore production Gills

Spores

Often appearing in crowds, the orange-brown caps open out flat, sporting radial lines and white tufts around their edges. The hollow stem is the same color and is covered with a fine, white frosting, a wispy ring, and fluffy white mycelium at the stem base.

Spore production
The gills connect fully to the stem in a matching color and have notable spaces between them while the spores are rust-brown, smooth-walled, and egg-shaped.

Sensory characteristics
Their smell is weakly mushroomy. Wispy tissue on the cap and stem can be washed away by rain or a curious gardener's finger. The color of the cap changes, getting paler as it dries.

FLUTED BIRD'S NEST

Scientific name
Cyathus striatus

Distribution
Widespread and common worldwide except polar regions

Habitat Woodchip or well-rotted wood

When to see Can occur any time of year but are most abundant in summer and fall

Type Stomach

Spore production Sac

Spores

Crowds of tiny, brown, nestlike cups that taper toward the base are initially covered with a white lid, with brown hairs on all sides. The lid peels away, revealing smooth, gray walls "fluted" with vertical ridges, and three or four silvery, lentil-shaped "eggs" inside.

Spore production
Each "egg" is a thin-walled sac filled with white, smooth, capsule-shaped spores, called peridioles. The sacs are moved by rain and animals, then release a mass of spores once their walls break down with age.

Sensory characteristics
The "eggs" are flung from the "nest" when raindrops fall on them.

HEARTWOOD

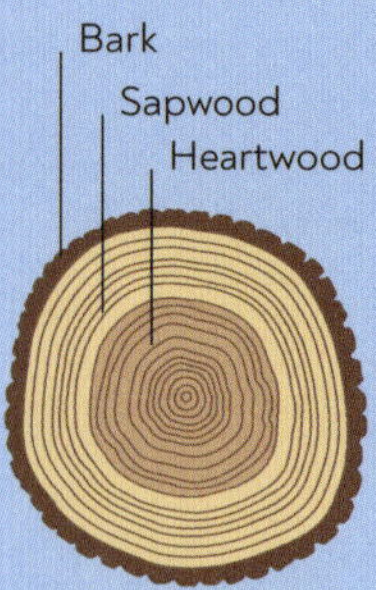

The heartwood of a tree can support a range of fungi.

Heartwood is the dense, inner part of a tree trunk that forms as a tree ages. The heartwood of mature trees contains a large reserve of dead wood. While sapwood contains living cells that transport water and nutrients to and from the roots and shoots, heartwood has served its duty and is now a pension pot of nutrients to withdraw in old age. This is where fungi come in.

What fungi do to heartwood

It takes many years for fungi to establish within heartwood. By the time a fruiting body appears, the mycelium in the wood has been establishing for years or decades. Fungi grow in all plant tissues, but healthy wood is filled with water and lacks oxygen, which fungal activity relies on. Fungi within heartwood grow slowly until the wood is damaged and aerated. Then they break the wood down for food. The resulting rot can be soft, white, or brown, depending on the type of fungi.

Benefits to wildlife

Fungi create hollows in trees that provide wildlife with habitats and hunting grounds, and the excess nutrition liberated by fungal digestion feeds wildlife and plants, including the tree itself. This happens when soft, rotted wood eventually falls away from the tree and makes its way back to the soil as soft sawdust, where it is further digested by wildlife and other microbes to form humus, creating a nutrient-rich soil.

Tree aging

Aging trees naturally acquire heartwood decay but are often cut down needlessly, meaning too few trees reach old age. Hollow trees are light and flexible so can better withstand strong winds, but if rot is badly positioned, it may create weak spots. Qualified arborists can assess tree strength and follow sensitive management practices to keep old trees standing for as long as possible to maintain these precious habitats.

The position and extent of heartwood decay determines the risk of breakage, so monitor old and decaying trees for their safety.

CHICKEN OF THE WOODS

Scientific name
Laetiporus sulphureus

Distribution Widespread and common in most temperate latitudes

Habitat Heartwood of mainly oak but sometimes yew, cherry, sweet chestnut, and willow

When to see
Early summer to fall

Type Polypore

Spore production Pores

Spores

Chicken of the woods has stacks of plump, undulating, sulfur-yellow fans with white interior flesh and orange bands on top. With age, the bracket edges grow thin, the colors turn pale, and the flesh becomes brittle and crumbly. Its mycelium causes brown cubical rot.

Spore production
The yellow underside is densely packed with roughly oval pores, fitting up to three per millimeter, which are the faces of tubes that are 3/8–1¼in (1–3cm) deep. The spores that they drop are white and smooth with a classic oval shape.

Sensory characteristics
Young growths smell pleasant and mushroomy and are a choice edible, but the scent and its edibility deteriorate with age. Specimens on yew trees may be unsafe to eat.

Supple and bright when young, becoming pale and brittle with age

Old brackets that eventually fall to the ground make excellent natural bird feeders.

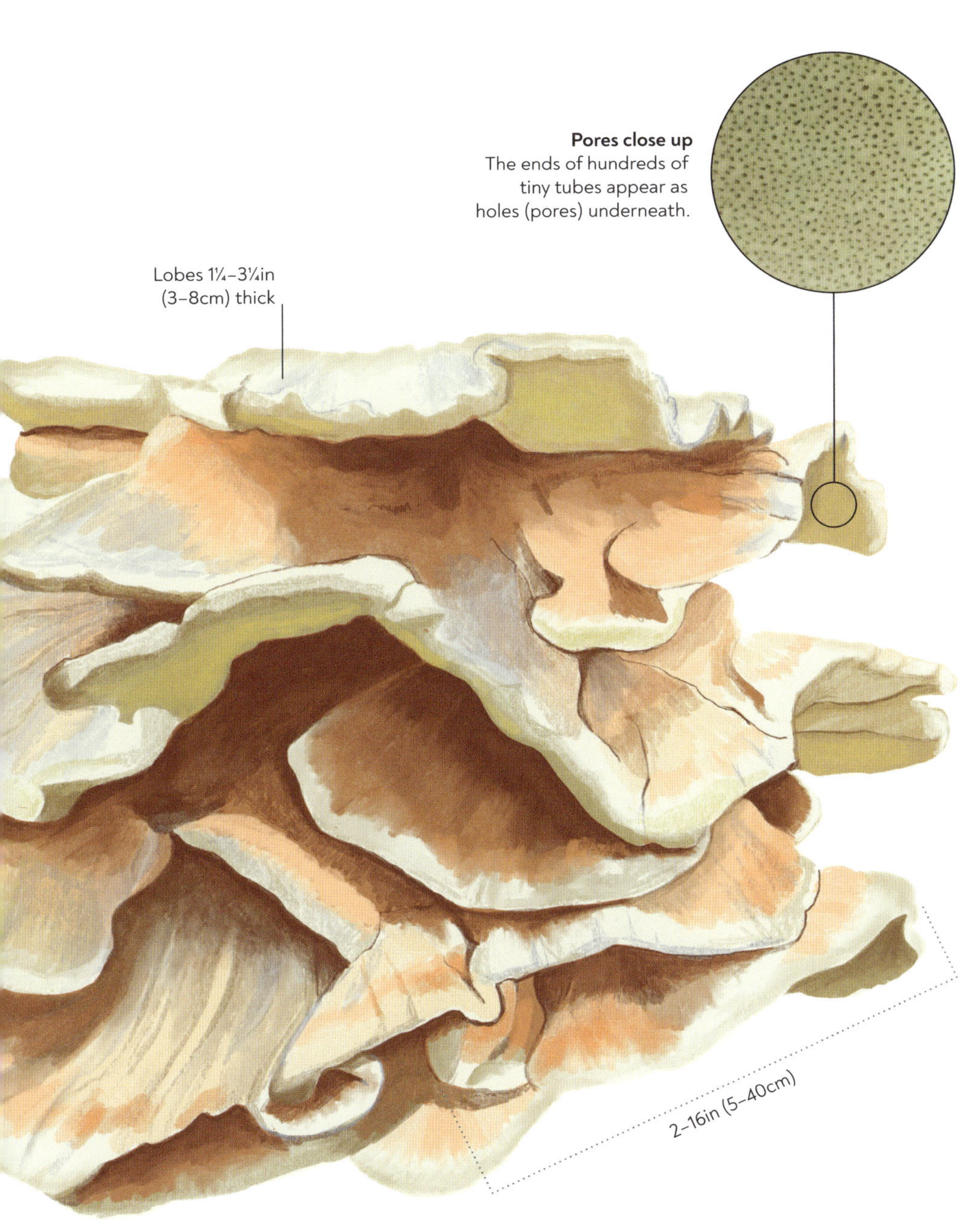
Pores close up
The ends of hundreds of
tiny tubes appear as
holes (pores) underneath.
Lobes 1¼–3¼in
(3–8cm) thick
2–16in (5–40cm)

SHAGGY BRACKET

Scientific name
Inonotus hispidus

Distribution Widespread and common in most temperate zones but rare farther north

Habitat High up heartwood of mainly old apple and ash trees

When to see Midsummer to late fall

Type Polypore

Spore production Pores

Spores

What begins as a peachy dome grows into a tough, clam-shell shape with a fuzzy, orange-brown top. The internal flesh is pale, but darkens once cut. The top color becomes darker with age and eventually the whole structure turns black, either staying attached to the tree for months or falling to the ground, where a tiny, white mushroom (*Collybia cookei*) may grow on it. Its mycelium usually creates white rot in dead wood of small garden trees, but it can damage sapwood and form bark cankers.

Spore production
The underside is cream at first, turning rusty with age, featuring dense pores, two to three per millimeter, which lead to tubes up

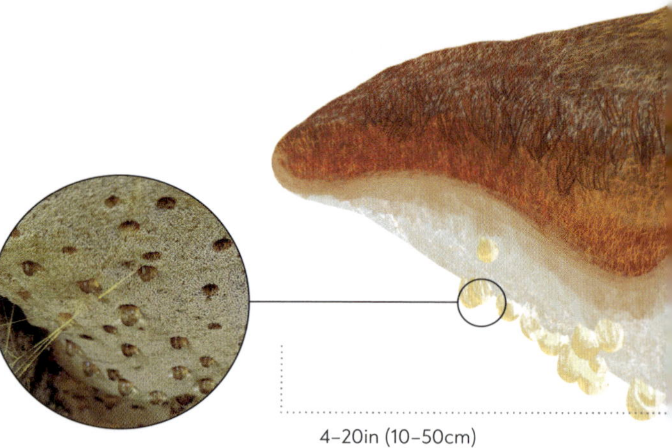

Suncatchers
Droplets fall from the underside of the bracket, catching the light.

Common in gardens on old apple trees, high on the trunk or at branching points.

to 1¼in (3cm) deep. From these pores, almost round yellow spores are dropped, which have thick, smooth walls.

Sensory characteristics
Clear to reddish liquid drips from underneath. Once dropped, the bright yellow spores may be visible on spiders' webs hanging below.

Color change
Over time, the shaggy bracket turns black, eventually falling to the ground.

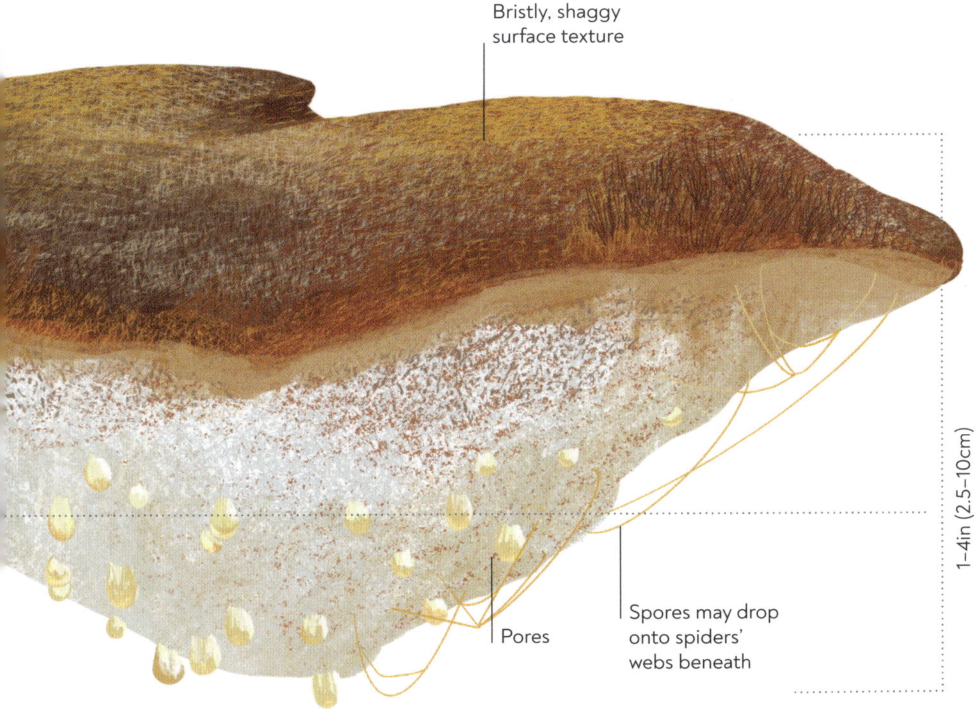

Bristly, shaggy surface texture

1–4in (2.5–10cm)

Pores

Spores may drop onto spiders' webs beneath

ARTIST'S CONK

Scientific name
G. applanatum

Distribution Widespread and common worldwide, excluding the far north for *G. australe*

Habitat Heartwood of deciduous trees

When to see All year

Type Polypore

Spore production
Pores

Spores

This fungi makes perennial clam-shell fruiting bodies that grow a bigger layer each year. The top is a lumpy, dull brown, and brittle crust with a white edge. Its brown inner flesh is very tough and the mycelia cause white rot.

Spore production
White very fine pores underneath (four to six per millimeter) are the freshest growth and conceal a layer of red-brown tubes, up to 2¾in (7cm) deep, which produce the spores. Tube layers are separated by fleshy layers. They drop small cocoa-colored oval spores with a granular texture inside a clear outer wall.

Sensory characteristics
The white pores bruise dark brown, neatly, and immediately when touched. Sometimes it also plays host to the larvae of the yellow flat-footed flay (*Agathomiya wankowiczii*) forming moundlike galls underneath.

BLACK-STAINING POLYPORE

Scientific name
Meripilus giganteus

Distribution Widespread and common in North America, particularly in temperate forests

Habitat Heartwood of deciduous tree roots, mainly beech

When to see Late summer to fall

Type Polypore

Spore production Pores

Spores

The pliant, beige, fan-shaped lobes of the black-staining polypore are banded with brown and creased on top. Internally, the flesh is cream-colored. Multiple large rosettes can appear at once, especially on cut stumps. The mycelium causes white rot in roots and a short distance up the trunk. Affected trees have hollow roots making them prone to being uprooted in high winds, until trees form extra buttress roots for reinforced stability.

Spore production
The cream underside contains a shallow layer of tubes, which open into fine pores, three to five per millimeter, which drop white, smooth, round spores.

Sensory characteristics
The fruiting body has a mushroomy scent and bruises black when handled and damaged.

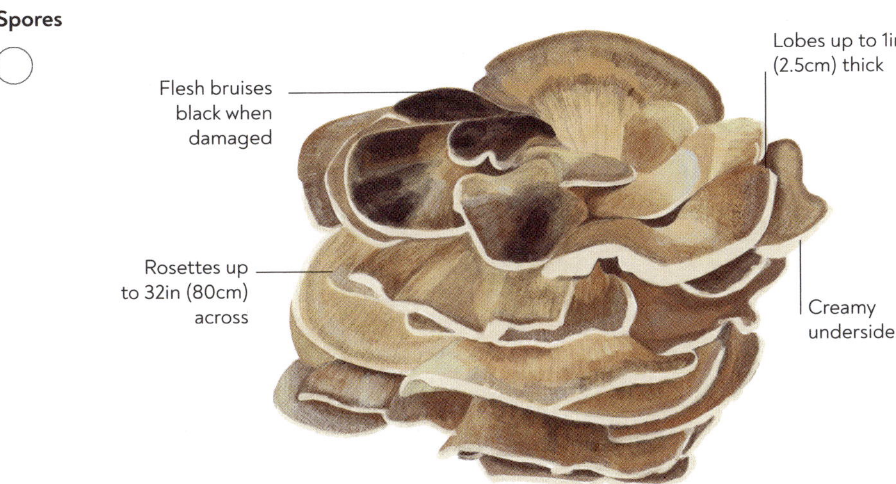

DEAD TREES

By the time a healthy tree dies from old age, it will have accrued a bustling assortment of life-forms that depend on it. If the tree is felled, the conditions change and so will this community of associates. Preserving these habitats is crucial to combat the biodiversity crisis.

Unmatched value

Standing dead trees are referred to as "monoliths," a rightly grandiose name. Dead trees have similar benefits to gardens as living, hollow trees, but the entire structure can be recycled to nourish soils and plants, and the range of wildlife it supports reaches its maximum. Different microhabitats develop—small to large cavities in the trunk, bark tears or bleeds, tree branches stripped of their bark, and decaying roots beneath the ground—that suit a range of fungi, other microbes, and wildlife. Flowering plants see huge benefits as dead trees provide the perfect habitats for pollinating insects like solitary bees, butterflies, hoverflies, and beetles.

Fungi on dead trees

Standing trees, living and dead, catch billions of fungal spores on their bark that get washed toward the ground by rain, increasing fungal diversity in the garden. Heartwood fungi that were present when the tree was alive will continue to decay the heartwood when the tree dies, and the dead sapwood can also now be degraded. Some of the fungal species known to be at risk of extinction, like bearded tooth,

Keeping old, dead trees standing for as long as possible provides rare and valuable habitats for fungi and wildlife.

also known as lion's mane (*Hericium erinaceus*), and oak polypore (*Buglossoporus quercinus*), rely on this rare habitat. Many more of the species that live in dead wood never make fruiting bodies, so can be detected only by analyzing the fungal DNA in wood samples.

SULPHUR TUFT

Scientific name
Hypholoma fasciculare

Distribution Widespread and common almost everywhere except the polar regions

Habitat Dead trunks, stumps, or buried roots of deciduous or conifer trees

When to see Spring and fall

Type Mushroom

Spore production Gills

Spores

Sulphur tuft grows in large clumps of domed yellow-orange caps on roughly textured stems 1¼–4¾in (3–12cm) in height, which are yellow, fading into brown at the base where it attaches to thick white cords of mycelium. They sometimes have wisps of tissue on the cap edges or near the top of the stem, forming a faint ring.

Spore production
Tightly packed, yellow-green gills that attach to the stem drop very dark, purple-black spores that are smooth ovals.

Sensory characteristics
The dark spores can be seen within a clump of mushrooms as the higher caps drop spores on lower caps.

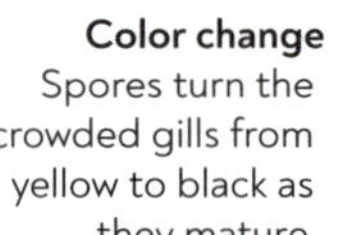

Color change
Spores turn the crowded gills from yellow to black as they mature.

Wood rotting
Sulphur tuft feeds on dead tree stumps and trunks. It will fruit regularly for several years before the wood is completely decayed.

The dark spore color and lack of a substantial ring of tissue on the stem helps distinguish these beneficial lookalikes from harmful honey fungus.

Caps measure ¾–2¾in (2–7cm) across

Sulfur-yellow caps with orange centers

Stems are ⅙–⅜in (4–10mm) thick

MICA CAP

Scientific name
Coprinellus micaceus

Distribution Widespread and very common across all latitudes except the polar regions

Habitat Dead trunks, stumps, and buried roots of broadleaved trees

When to see All year round

Type Mushroom

Spore production Gills

Spores

These clusters of tan-brown caps are heavily pleated from center to edge and coated with specks of residue on top that glisten like crystals. The caps open into a bell-shape set over slender white finely, hairy stems.

Spore production
Smooth, dark brown-black spores shaped like a bishop's hat are released by dissolving gills, which at first are white, tightly packed, and detached from the stem.

Sensory characteristics
The glistening residues are easily shed. The black inky spores help distinguish this from honey fungus, which has white spores.

¾–2in (2–5cm)

1½–3¼in (4–8cm)

Glistening residue

Stems up to ¼in (6mm) thick

BIRCH POLYPORE

Scientific name
Fomitopsis betulina

Distribution Widespread and common in most of the northern hemisphere

Habitat Dead or dying birch trees and logs

When to see All year; fresh growth in late summer

Type Polypore

Spore production Pores

Spores

This annual polypore first emerges as a white-gray bulb then flattens out into a chubby clamshell, tapering where it meets the wood. The top turns matte brown and is often cracked and mottled, revealing the white inner flesh, which is tough with a little give at first but becomes brittle and crumbly with age.

Spore production
Underneath, a thin layer of fine white tubes open, forming tiny pores (three to five per millimeter), which drop white, smooth-walled spores shaped like slightly curved, thin sausages.

Sensory characteristics
Both the top layer of tissue and the tube layer easily peel away from the internal flesh. Peeled tissue from the top is sticky where it meets the flesh. It even has antiseptic properties and can be wrapped over a wound to act as a temporary plaster.

FALLEN WOOD

Felled and fallen wood is slowly transformed by the fungi that feed on it. Thinner pieces of wood are favored by different fungi over those that thrive on thicker logs. Many fungi are trapped on its bark as spores or grow in the wood as mycelium. Other fungi may enter the wood from the soil.

The presence of any wood on the ground helps maintain moisture levels in the soil, but the sides where the wood contacts the ground stay the wettest and so experience the most rapid fungal decay (see pp22–23).

The fruiting bodies found on dead wood include some that are less recognizable as fungi, such as jellies, crusts, and charcoal fungi, as well as more familiar types. Jellies can be misidentified as slime molds or resin deposits, while crusts and charcoal fungi often lie flat against the wood, hiding in plain sight.

Fruiting bodies on smaller twigs often appear from snapped ends or through leaf scars. They are easier to inspect as you can bring the twig up to eye level.

Changing direction

Perennial fruiting bodies on standing wood that later falls to the ground, begin growing in a different orientation because fungi have the ability to sense and react to gravity. New spore-producing layers grow parallel to the ground as this gives the most effective spore dispersal.

Fruiting bodies can be found by rolling rotting logs, although do so infrequently and roll them back afterward to minimize any disturbance.

Log piles can be hot spots
of fruiting bodies
Keep stumps as long
as the tree didn't die
of root disease
Jellies often grow
on log piles
Sticks and twigs
support different
fungi to thicker wood

TURKEY TAIL

Scientific name
Trametes versicolor

Distribution Widespread and extremely common worldwide except the polar regions

Habitat Dead, fallen wood of deciduous trees

When to see All year

Type Polypore

Spore production Pores

Spores

Turkey tail usually appears in large groups in crowded tiers on cut or fallen wood. Velvety tops feature concentric stripes resembling a turkey's tail in variable shades of brown, tinged with colors ranging from orange to blue, and are rimmed with white. These slim annual brackets last for months. At first tough, they eventually become pale and crumbly.

Spore production
Tiny pores are packed into the white lower layer, with four to five per millimeter, which drop white spores shaped like rice grains.

Sensory characteristics
The scent is pleasant and mushroomy. It was used traditionally in medicinal tinctures.

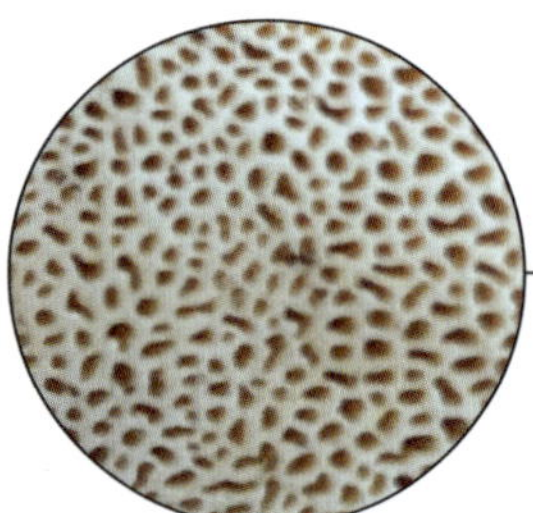

Pores
Look closely at the white underside to spot these tiny holes.

Their variable nature means that it is always a marvel to see each unique banding pattern.

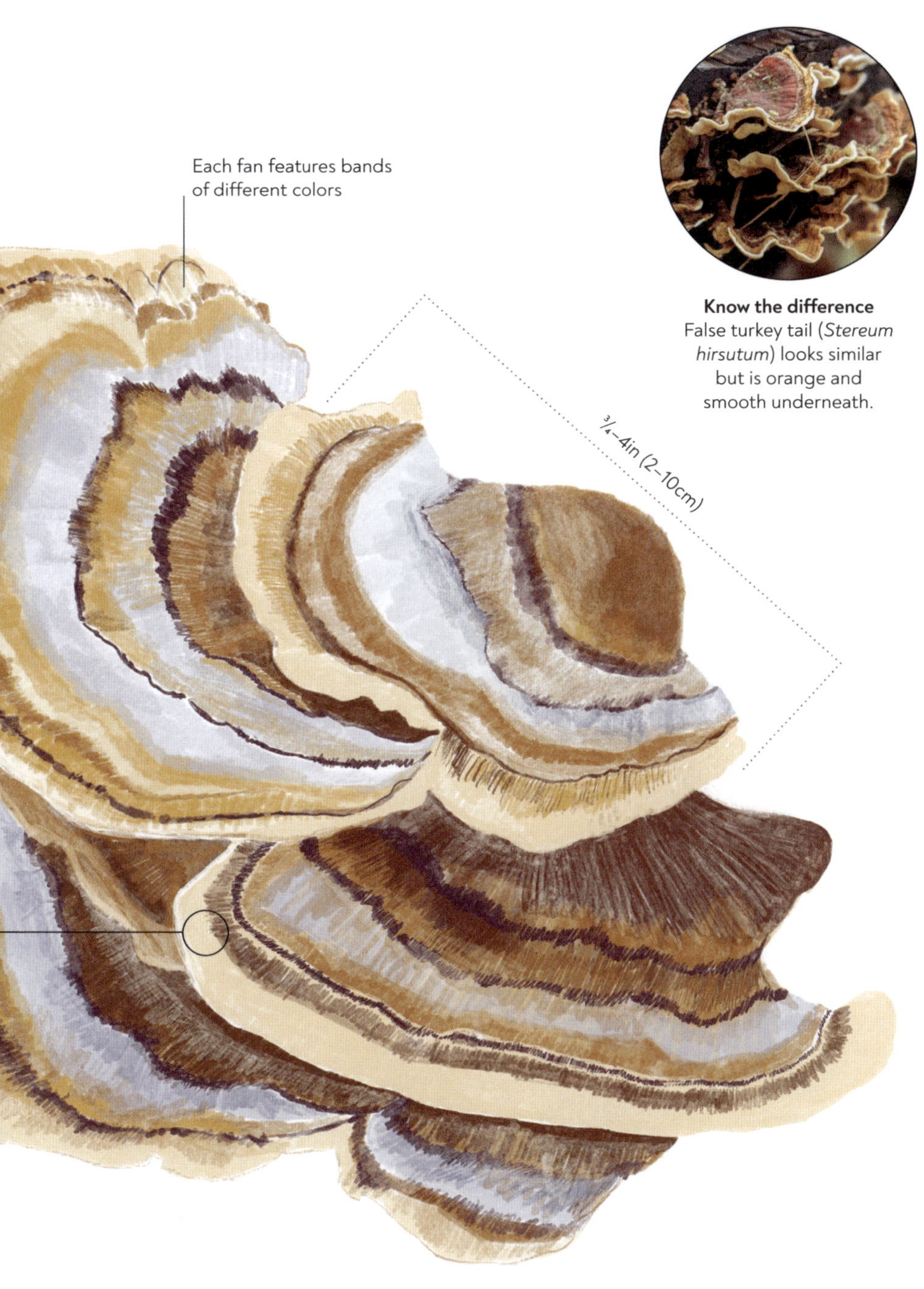

Know the difference
False turkey tail (*Stereum hirsutum*) looks similar but is orange and smooth underneath.

JELLY EAR

Scientific name
Auricularia auricula-judae

Distribution Widespread but commonly found in Europe, Asia, and North America

Habitat Dead wood of elder or other deciduous trees

When to see All year, peaking in winter

Type Jelly

Spore production On the surface

Spores

This is a "jelly fungus," a term that refers to the wobbly characteristic of the fruiting bodies. Starting out as rounded domes, the fruiting bodies expand into lobed, wrinkled flaps of tissue that look spookily like human ears. The outer side is colored translucent purple-brown, while the inside is paler. Historically, this fungus fruited only on wood of the elder tree but is now found on species, including ash, hazel, and willow, potentially due to the changing climate.

Spore production
The paler, concave surface carries the spores, which are formed on the outside of the surface and drop away. The spore print is white and spores are shaped like bendy sausages.

Sensory characteristics
The "ears" are velvety on the outer side. In dry weather or if picked, they will dry out but will return to their former glory when rehydrated.

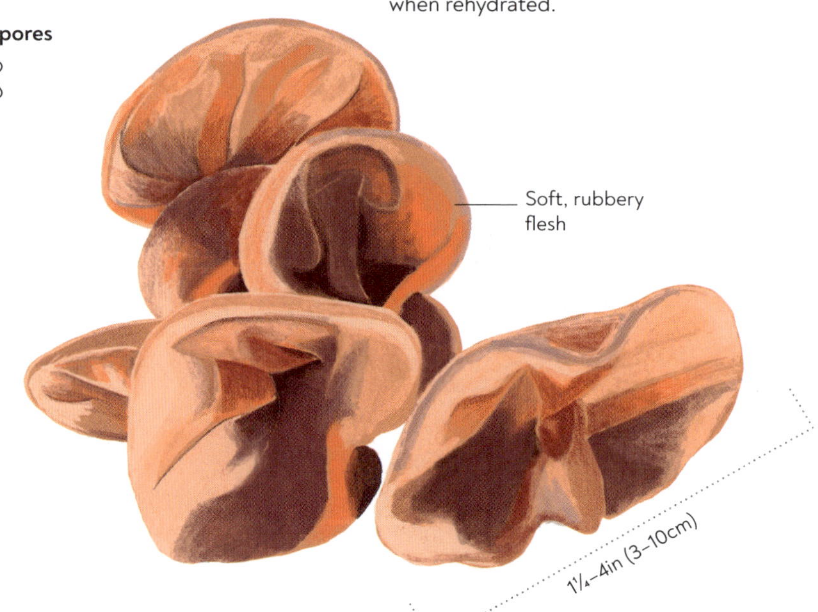

CANDLESNUFF

Scientific name
Xylaria hypoxylon

Distribution Widespread and common worldwide

Habitat Rotting logs or stumps of mainly deciduous but occasionally conifer wood

When to see All year

Type Charcoal fungus

Spore production On and within the surface

Spores

These tough "charcoal fungi" are so named because they appear like burnt wood. Crowds of slender upright spikes appear along logs or dead branches. Candlesnuff is often forked like antlers with black outer and white inner flesh.

Spore production
Apart from a short section at the base, the surface is usually coated with white, powdery, asexual spores (conidia) that are smooth-walled and spindle-shaped. In fall, these surfaces turn black and bumpy. A tiny hole opens in each bump, releasing larger black, smooth, bean-shaped sexual spores (ascospores).

Sensory characteristics
Flick a spike when white to see spores escape as a white cloud of dust. In fall, when blackened, cut one lengthwise to see the minute chambers (perithecia) beneath the bumps, each filled with black spores.

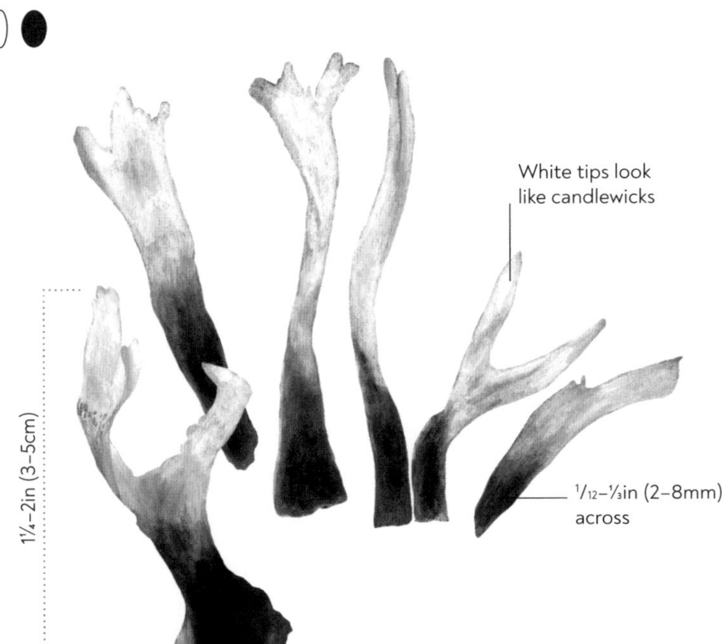

LEAF LITTER

Green leaves held aloft on plants are pebble-dashed by wind-blown spores. When the leaves die, any recycler fungi that were able to survive on the leaf surface or internally can rot down and feed on their tissues. Recycler fungi in the soil or existing leaf litter will also make moves to colonize freshly fallen leaves. Collectively, these fungi digest complex plant polymers, then work together with bacterial and animal decomposers to complete the breakdown process.

In one to three years' time, a fresh carpet of dead leaves will be transformed into new humus. The rate of decay varies with different combinations of leaves and fungi, and leaf litter will rot down faster in the location it grew in than if it is moved elsewhere—another advantage of making your own leaf mold (see p100).

Specialist fungi

In fall when most leaves fall, many fungi make their fruiting bodies. The fungi that have rotted leaves from previous seasons will be well fed from this process, but as the leaf disappears, so does their food source. By producing fruiting bodies, their spores will settle onto freshly fallen leaves and carry on their life cycle.

You may need to brush the top leaves away to spot fruiting bodies concealed by the newly shed leaves. Bonnet fungi (*Mycena*) make cone-capped tiny mushrooms that may smell of radishes or have a colored outline on their gills. The parachute fungi (*Marasmius*) make mushrooms that are often even smaller than bonnet species. Checking on which leaves each fruiting body is growing from will help determine its identity.

The fungi that fruit directly on fallen leaves are often tiny, but their fragility also makes them exquisitely beautiful.

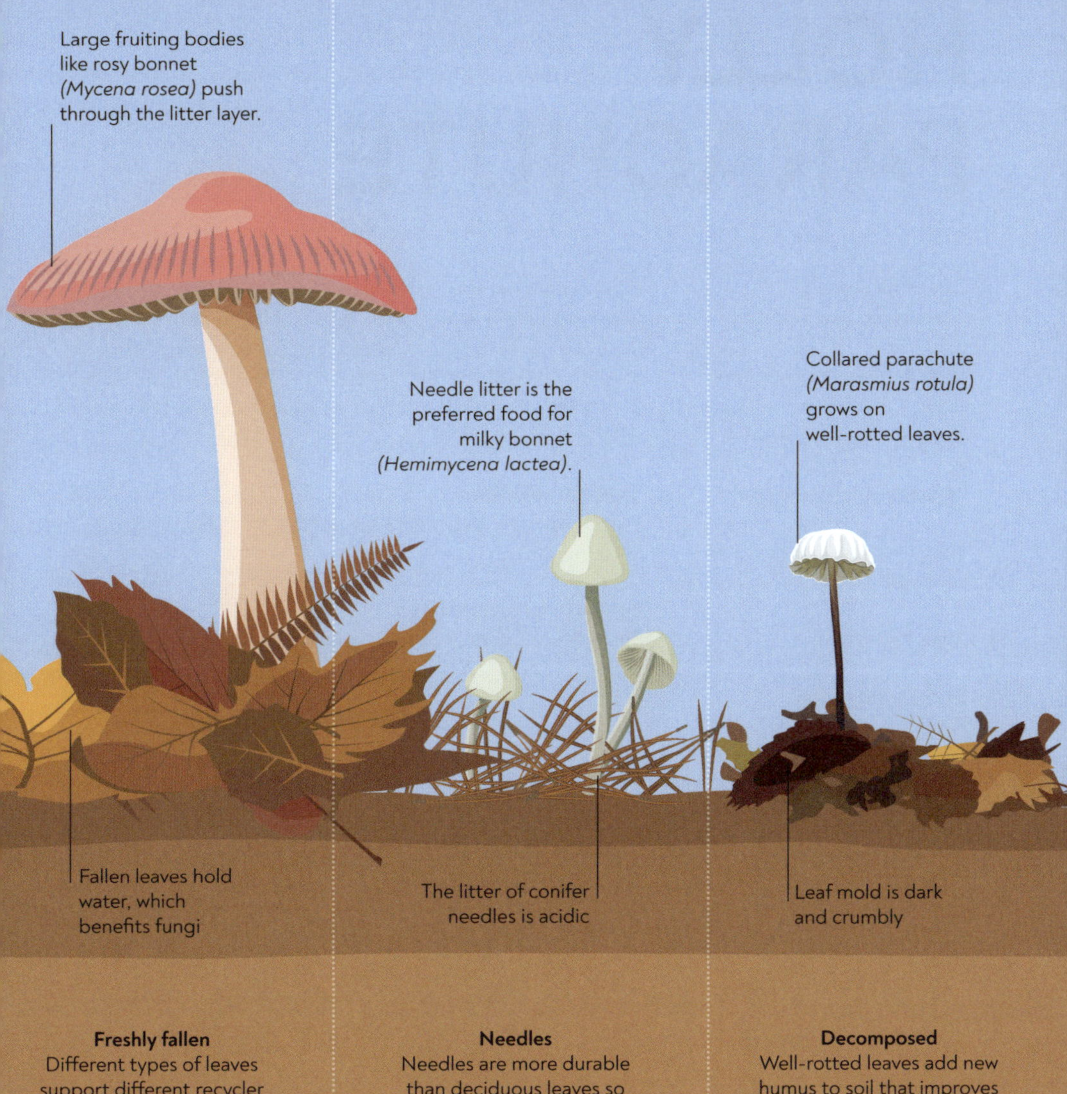

Freshly fallen
Different types of leaves support different recycler fungi. Some species grow exclusively on a single kind of leaf, while others have a broader diet.

Needles
Needles are more durable than deciduous leaves so take longer to decay.

Decomposed
Well-rotted leaves add new humus to soil that improves its structure and moisture-holding properties.

HOLLY PARACHUTE

Scientific name
Marasmius hudsonii

Distribution Occasional in Britain, rare in southern Europe, absent elsewhere

Habitat Dead holly leaves

When to see Late summer to winter

Type Mushroom

Spore production
Gills

Spores

These exquisite, tiny mushrooms grow exclusively on dead holly leaves, usually in groups of up to five. Their pale, hemispherical caps are 1/12–¼in (2–6mm) across and hoisted up on relatively long wiry stems. The stems are mostly dark brown but fade to match the cap just before they meet and can also be covered with red-brown hairs.

Spore production
Wide, pale gills make white, smooth spores shaped like a narrow pip.

Sensory characteristics
The spiky hairs are too small to feel prickly to the touch. They make good subject material for a macrophotography project.

Dead, moist holly leaves make a home for this tiny mushroom

The genus *Marasmius* is so named for being able to withstand drying and rehydrating as the Greek word *marasmos* means "drying out."

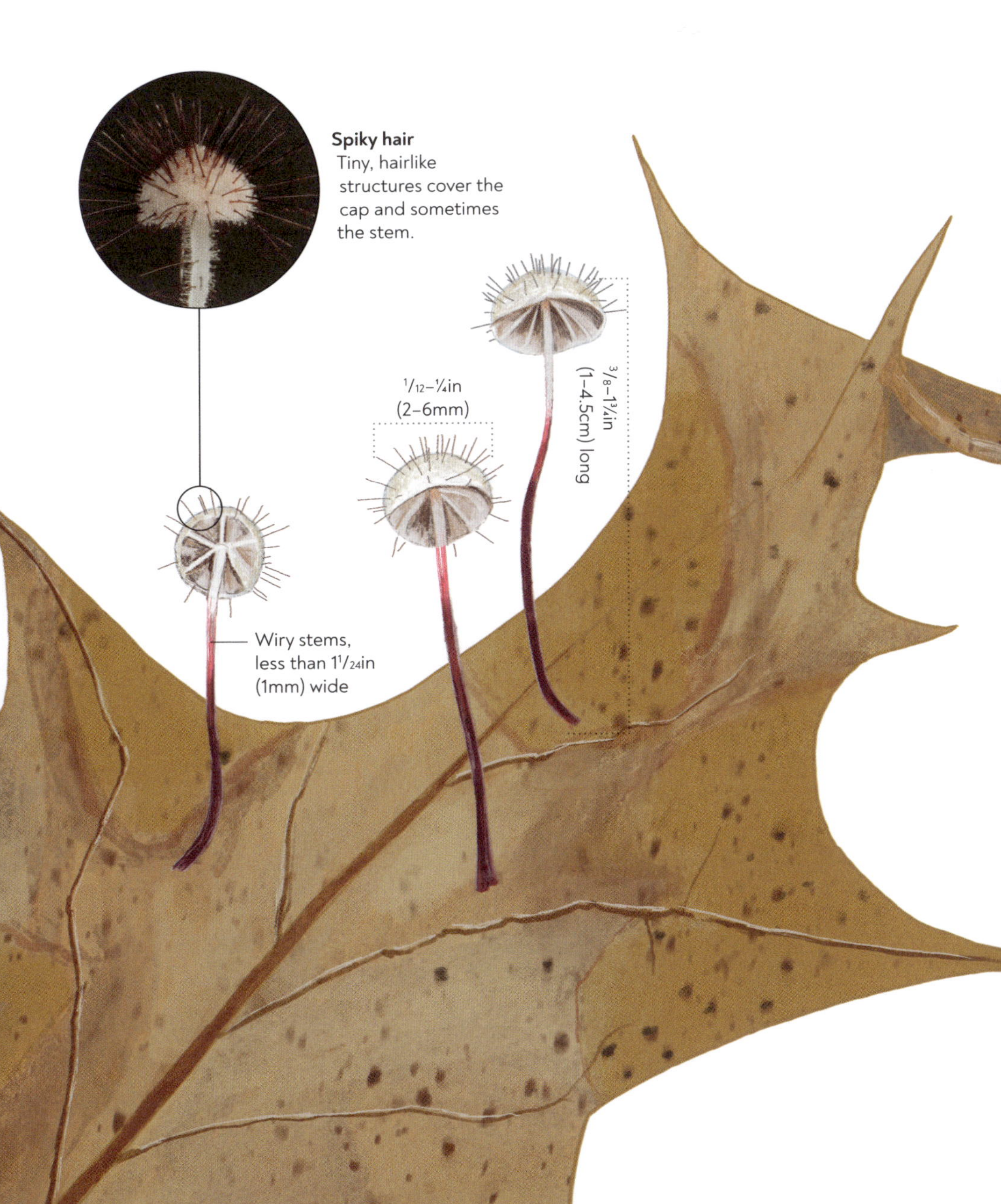

Spiky hair
Tiny, hairlike structures cover the cap and sometimes the stem.
1/12–1/4in
(2–6mm)
3/8–1 3/4in
(1–4.5cm) long
Wiry stems, less than 1 1/24in (1mm) wide

COLLARED EARTHSTAR

Scientific name
Geastrum michelianum (formerly *G. triplex*)

Distribution Widespread and occasional in Europe

Habitat Leaf litter, needle litter, and compost

When to see Early fall to midwinter

Type Stomach

Spore production Sac

Spores

Tan-brown spheres are enclosed in a thick outer layer that splits open to reveal its pale, gray-brown lining. A fluffy, protruding opening on top is ringed by a pale halo. The segments of outer skin curl back on themselves, lifting the fruiting body up. The pale inner lining of the skin cracks into a collar around the inner sac.

Spore production
Dark olive-brown, spiky, round spores form in the spherical sac and are forced upward through the opening when the sac is disturbed by raindrops or wildlife.

Sensory characteristics
Poke the sac to release a plume of dark spores.

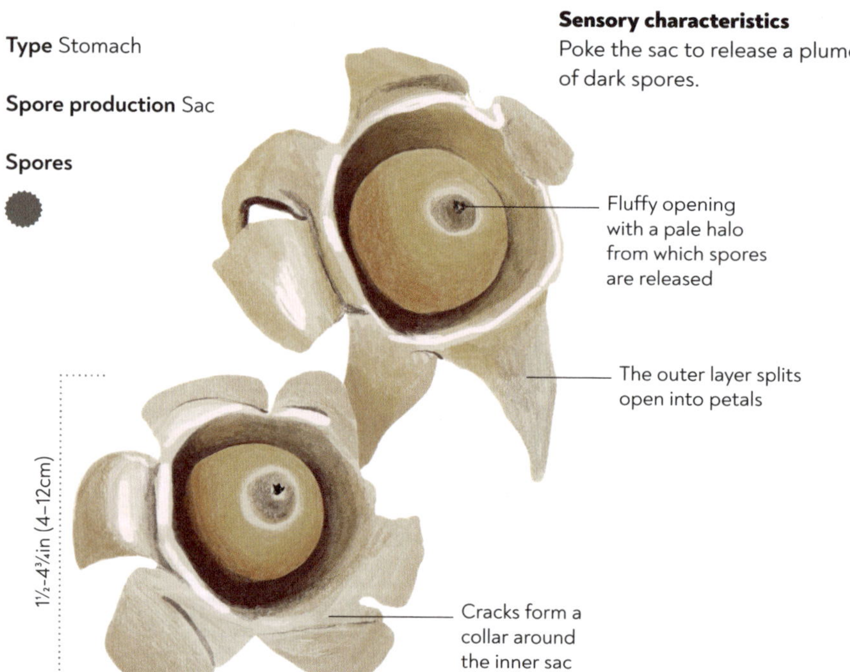

WOOD BLEWIT

Scientific name *Collybia nuda* (formerly *Lepista*)

Distribution Widespread and common in the northern hemisphere, introduced to and increasing in Australia

Habitat Leaf litter beside paths or hedges

When to see
Fall to winter

Type Mushroom

Spore production Gills

Spores

These purple-brown, wavy caps are fleshy and thick. The stem is fleshy likewise and gets wider toward the base, colored uniformly lilac with a fibrous texture. The firm flesh is marbled lilac-gray inside.

Spore production
Tightly packed lilac gills are joined to the stem by a tiny section and drop pink-brown, rough-textured, oval spores.

Sensory characteristics
Their perfumed smell is sometimes described as frozen orange juice. Its cap color becomes slightly darker with increased moisture content. Blewits are edible when cooked but can cause allergic reactions to those that are sensitive to them. Their appearance strongly resembles poisonous webcaps (*Cortinarius* species), but the different spore colors reliably tell them apart (pastel pink-brown for blewits versus bright orange-brown for webcaps).

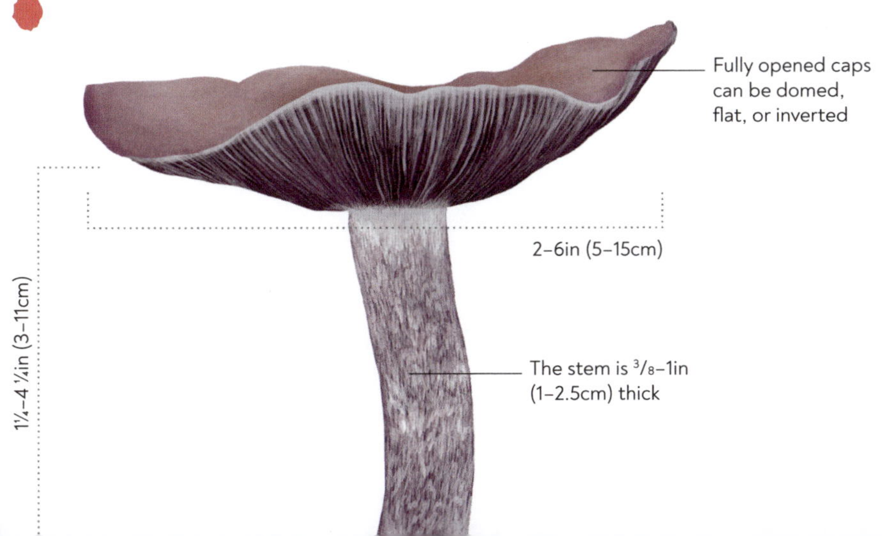

GRASS AND LAWNS

Fungi fruiting in lawns vary from muted mushrooms that blend into the sward to imposing giant forms. But most lawns are relatively lacking in fungi and the liveliest fungal communities dwell in long-established mossy, mixed-species lawns with no soil disturbance or nutritional inputs.

Minimal interference

The richest fungal habitats are unimproved grasslands, and it takes decades to build up the most precious fungal communities that feature the flamboyant waxcaps, earthtongues, pinkgills, corals, and crazed caps (collectively known as CHEGD fungi). The short tenure of a gardener of any patch of turf means few will accrue these treasured fungi at home, but it is well worth creating an unimproved grassy area in hope that it may continue after your time.

FAIRY RINGS

Feeding lawns with anything (synthetic and organic alike) deters fungi from establishing there.

Unlike leaf litter and dead wood habitats, it is better for fungi when grass clippings are composted instead of leaving them on top of the lawn. Leave time between mowings for fungi to succeed.

Fairy rings

One of the most remarkable formations you can see growing in lawns is a fairy ring. As mycelium grows outward in all directions in search of food from an initial single point underground, a ring of fruiting bodies appears. In some cases, the growth habit of the grass is changed by these rings of fruiting bodies, becoming more lush or bare depending on fungal activity.

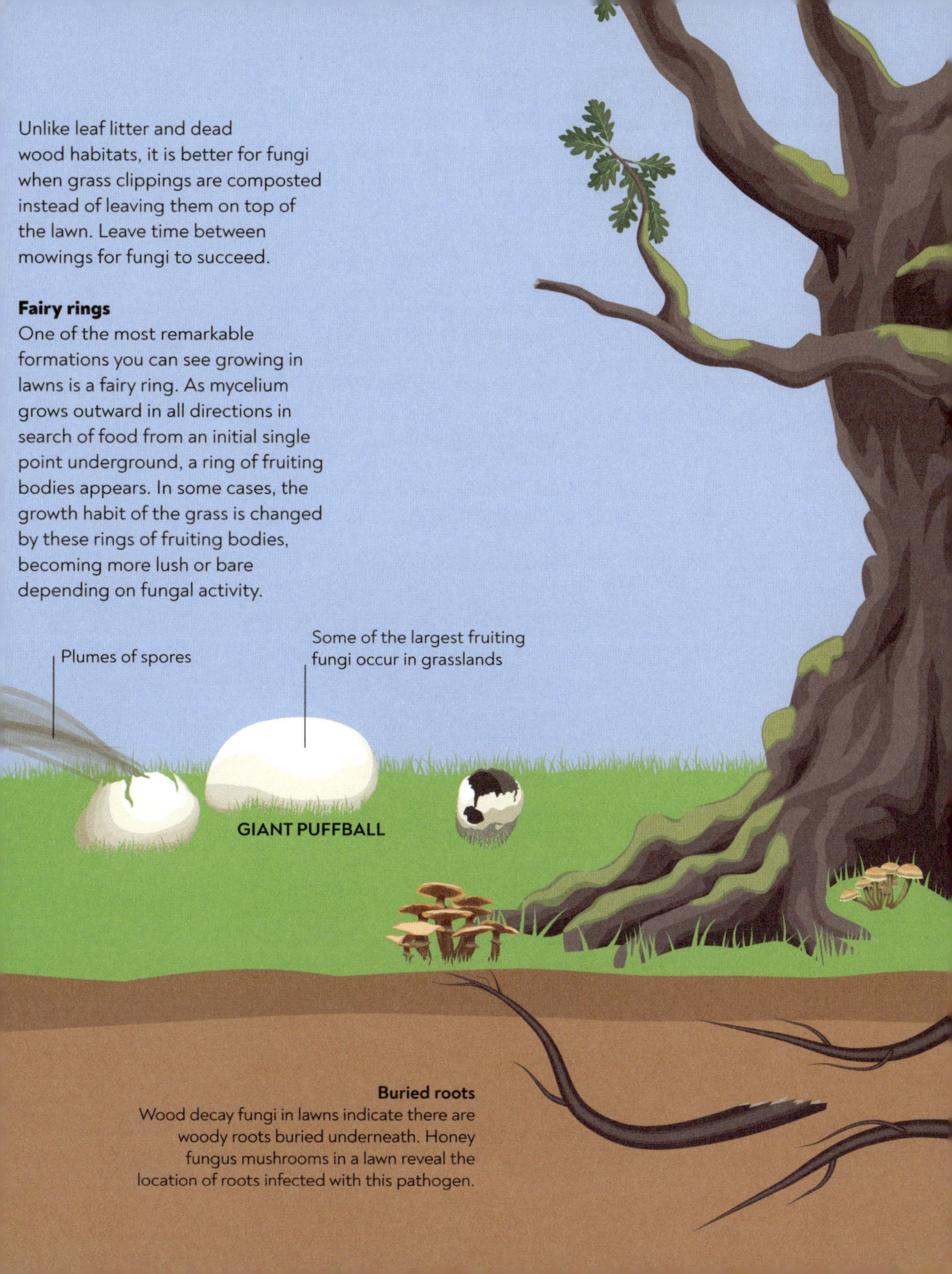

Buried roots

Wood decay fungi in lawns indicate there are woody roots buried underneath. Honey fungus mushrooms in a lawn reveal the location of roots infected with this pathogen.

SHAGGY MANE

Scientific name
Coprinus comatus

Distribution Widespread and common everywhere

Habitat Grass verges and lawns

When to see Fall

Type Mushroom

Spore production Gills

Spores

These substantial mushrooms often appear in large groups and create an impressive display. Their long, narrow, white caps are covered with shaggy white tufts. The very tall, white, hollow stems have a ring that often falls to rest near the base.

Spore production
Tightly packed whitish gills are mostly free of the stem but rapidly turn black with the color of the smooth, oval spores as they mature.

Sensory characteristics
Their stems are very fragile and will collapse if handled. The caps never reach their potential diameter because they self-digest (deliquesce) as they age, leaving just a small island of flesh on top of the stem dripping ink-black spores.

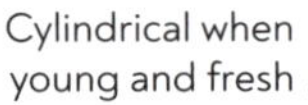

Fast-changing color
Within a week, the fluffy white caps morph into black inky liquid.

MAKE YOUR OWN INK

Cut caps and leave them in a tub for a day, then strain through cheesecloth to remove any lumps.

GIANT PUFFBALL

Scientific name
Calvatia gigantea

Distribution Widespread and occasional across all latitudes except the polar regions

Habitat Nutrient-rich grass or on compost

When to see Late summer to early fall

Type Stomach

Spore production Sac

Spores

A very large, approximately spherical fruiting body with a thin skin that starts white and smooth but grows dark and papery with age. The wrinkled base attaches to mycelium cords.

Spore production
The white tissue that fills the ball matures into a powdery mass of muddy brown spores that are round and covered with small bumps ("warts").

Sensory characteristics
They are edible when young and white throughout. The dusty spores escape once the skin splits open, but the skin around the base of old specimens may persist long after its contents have been shed. Poke one to see a dark cloud of spores billow out.

4–32in (10–80cm)

The surface is often pocked where animals have grazed on it

CHANGING SIZES

To give an idea of scale, if a yellow fieldcap was the size of a person, a giant puffball would be the size of a house.

YELLOW FIELDCAP

Scientific name
Bolbitius titubans

Distribution Widespread and common across most latitudes but rarer toward the polar regions

Habitat Meadows, lawns, or manured soil

When to see Any time of year, following rainfall

Type Mushroom

Spore production Gills

Spores

These small yellow caps are egg-shaped while closed around the fragile, hollow stem. The stem is whitish with a frosted texture. Over the course of a day, the caps open out flat and turn pale from the edges inward, the stems fall over, and the structure shrinks away.

Spore production
Cream-colored gills, not too tightly packed, that connect narrowly to the stem, drop cinnamon-colored, smooth-walled, oval spores.

Sensory characteristics
The young caps are covered with a sticky or slimy film of residue that gives them a glossy look that dries out to a satin sheen. The dramatic change in appearance includes a phase when the last of the yellow sits inside a white brim, giving the appearance of a tiny fried egg.

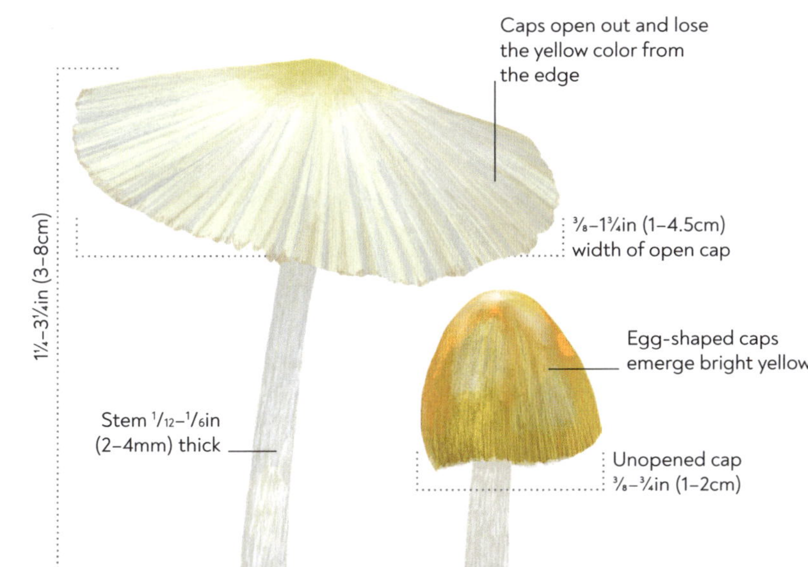

MOWER'S MUSHROOM

Scientific name
Panaeolina foenisecii

Distribution Widespread and common worldwide except in extreme polar regions

Habitat Meadows and lawns

When to see Late spring to late fall

Type Mushroom

Spore production Gills

Spores

These small caps are domed or bell-shaped and change color from dark brown to pale beige from the middle outward as they lose moisture. Their relatively long, thin stems are stiff, light brown, and sometimes have a frosted texture.

Spore production
Light brown gills are arranged in an alternating fashion with full gills that connect to the stem separated by shorter gills that do not. The dark brown, roughly textured spores are lemon-shaped. Spores are produced unevenly over the gill surfaces, creating a mottled effect.

Sensory characteristics
Mower's mushroom is neither edible nor toxic, despite rumors of their potential to poison children, which have been refuted by the evidence from case studies.

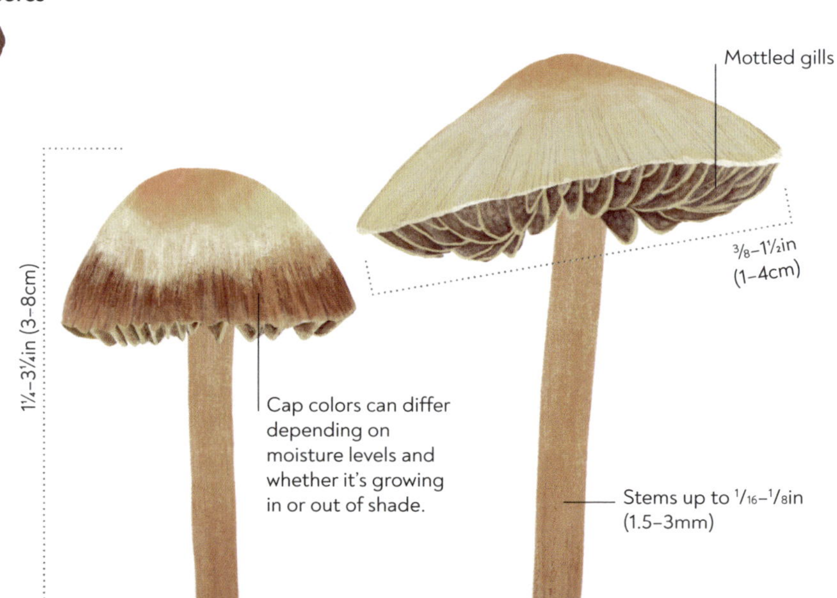

FAIRY RING MUSHROOM

Scientific name
Marasmius oreades

Distribution Widespread and very common worldwide except the polar regions

Habitat Grass and lawn, feeding on thatch or grass roots

When to see Late spring to late fall

Type Mushroom

Spore production Gills

Spores

These mushrooms create circular formations of buff, wavy caps. Each cap expands almost flat but for a wide central mound and may have a pleated edge. The slim and sturdy stem is covered in tiny hairs and is a similar color to the cap.

Spore production
Widely spaced, rather deep gills are only shallowly connected to the stem, colored pale buff. Its white, smooth spores are shaped like apple pips.

Sensory characteristics
The cap color of fairy ring mushrooms gets paler as it dries out. They have a distinctive scent reminiscent of bitter almonds or pleasant spices.

Lush grass
The grass beside the ring where the fungus is active becomes lush and green but then may turn brown temporarily.

SOIL

Whatever the soil type in your garden, it will be packed full of fungi. These communities include mycorrhizal fungi (see pp78–79), recycler fungi, and fungi that grow inside plants as endophytes. However, the true complexity of soil life is unknowable since many of the species within it cannot be grown in a laboratory. Scientists call soil a "black box" because of how hard it is to study, but we do know that a soil rich in fungi is a healthy one.

How fungi help soil

Growing as mycelia, fungi weave through soil particles, gently holding them in place to resist erosion and maintain air spaces. Many mycorrhizae produce a protein-based substance called glomalin, which is good for sticking microscopic specks of soil together and helps it retain water and resist pH changes and high temperatures. Mycelial networks also make soils more interconnected as they can transport resources, water, and signals across their lengths. Additionally, soil is enriched with the products of fungal nutrient recycling that support plant growth and microbes. Soil fauna, including bacteria and invertebrates like worms that break down nutrients and improve soil structure, are also supported.

The soil community

Soil communities are competitive, so any new arriving spores need the advantages of being adapted to the local conditions and flora if they are to become established. Plant pathogens often spend part of their life cycle in soils, although soils with good microbial diversity can suppress disease.

Fruiting bodies

Comparatively few soil fungi produce fruiting bodies, but to best appreciate those that do, you need to get down to ground level and take the "worm's-eye view." Peat-free potting compost often produces fruiting bodies, which is a good sign of nutrient cycling, but may mean it is being overwatered. An excess of fruiting bodies in seedling trays can obstruct seedlings—these can be picked off and watering reduced.

Most fungi dwell in the top few inches of soil, but many also occur deeper down.

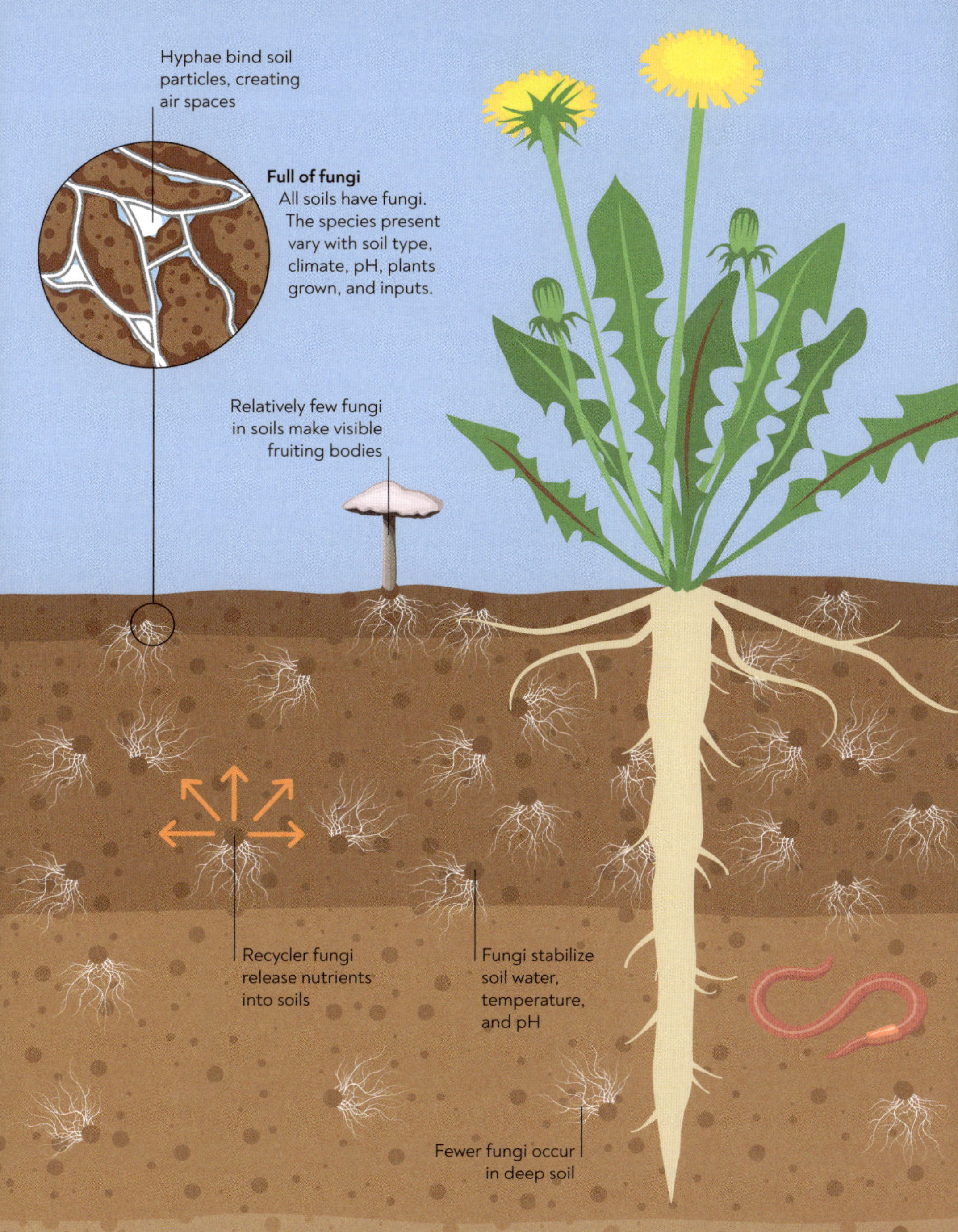
Hyphae bind soil particles, creating air spaces
Full of fungi
All soils have fungi. The species present vary with soil type, climate, pH, plants grown, and inputs.
Relatively few fungi in soils make visible fruiting bodies
Recycler fungi release nutrients into soils
Fungi stabilize soil water, temperature, and pH
Fewer fungi occur in deep soil

UPRIGHT CORAL

Scientific name
Ramaria stricta

Distribution Widespread and very common all over the northern hemisphere; occasional in southern hemisphere

Habitat Soil of mulched beds or on rotting wood

When to see Midsummer to late fall

Type Coral

Spore production
On its surface

Spores

The upright coral has dense, rubbery clumps of yellow-beige narrow tubes. It occurs where soils have been fed with woody debris, generating abundant white mycelium in the soil. If growing too vigorously, the mass of mycelium may create a water-repellent patch where plants struggle to absorb water, in which case you can break up the mycelial mass and add some extra compost.

Spore production
Sand-colored, bumpy-walled, lemon-shaped spores are released all over the tube surfaces.

Sensory characteristics
The flesh sometimes bruises dark red when damaged and has a slight scent reminiscent of aniseed or sour fruits.

The upright coral and its close relatives can adopt different roles, including mycorrhizal or recycler fungi.

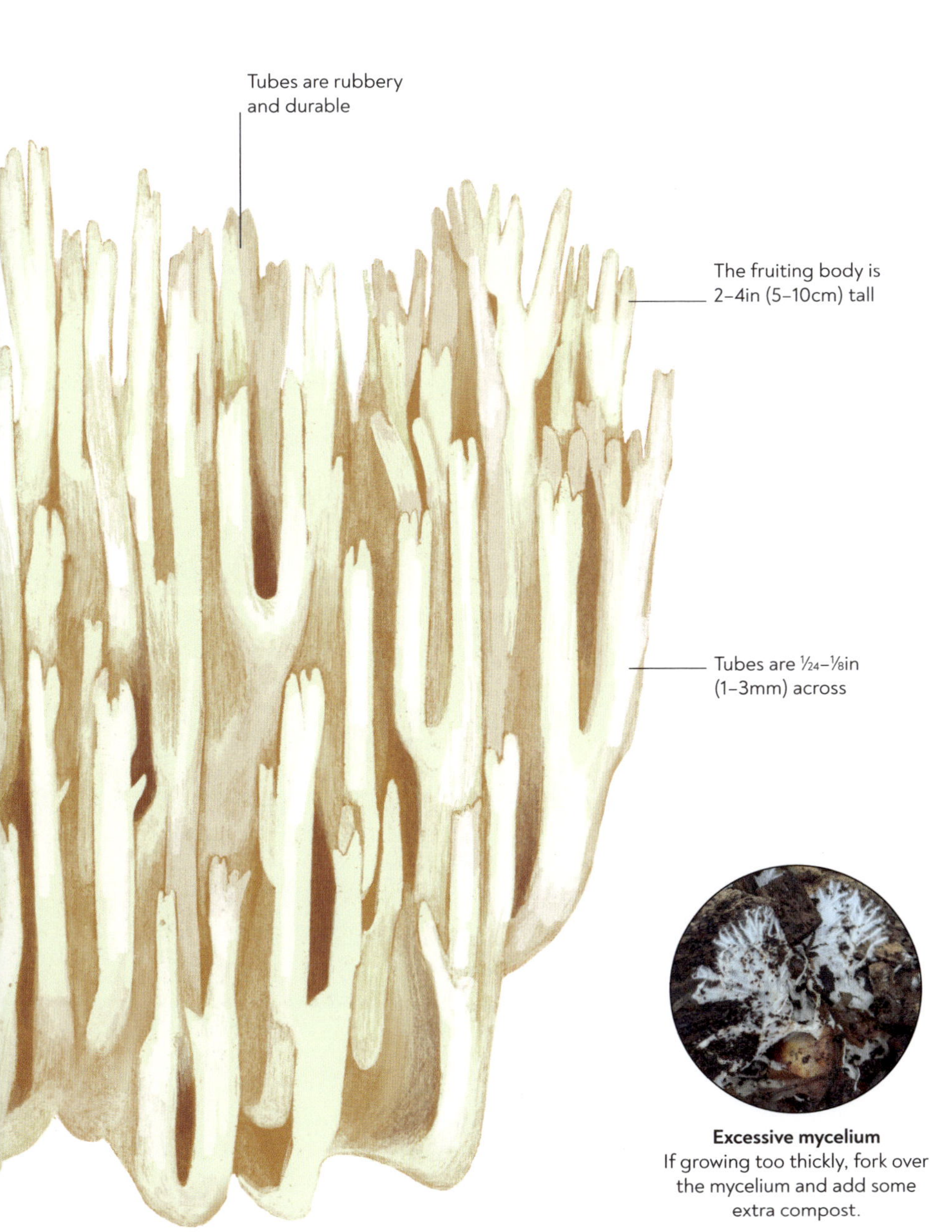

Excessive mycelium
If growing too thickly, fork over the mycelium and add some extra compost.

BLISTERED CUP

Scientific name
Peziza vesiculosa

Distribution Widespread and common across temperate latitudes, less frequent in boreal zones

When to see Any time of year but especially abundant in spring

Habitat Compost or manured soil

Type Cup

Spore production
Inner surface

Spores

Each shallow, beige cup varies in size and shape, with a rough, paler exterior, an in-rolled rim, and no stem. They appear in groups directly on the soil and their shapes can be warped when pressed against their neighbors. If masses of cups grow on top of seedlings, shading them out, remove the cups by hand and reduce watering.

Spore production
The smooth, inner beige surface is lined with spore-producing cells that shoot out white, smooth-walled, oval spores.

Sensory characteristics
Rain or wind stimulate the spore-shooting mechanism. Blow on a cup to trigger a puff of spores.

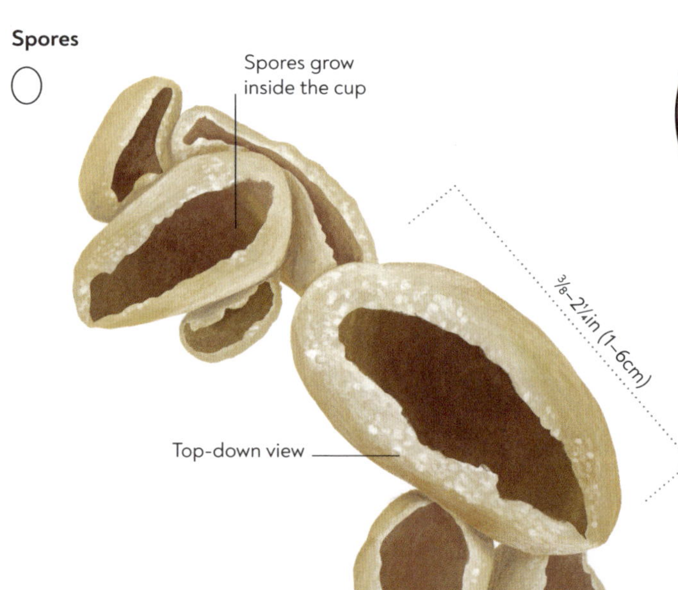

Clustered growth
Blistered cup, also known as common dung cup, thrives on manure and compost.

STINKHORN

Scientific name *Phallus impudicus*

Distribution Widespread and very common in temperate latitudes in the northern hemisphere

Habitat Soil often next to rotting conifer wood

When to see Summer to early winter

Type Stomach

Spore production Liquid on cap surface

Spore

Beginning as a white, tough ball embedded in the soil surface, bell-shaped caps emerge. Their white flesh is puckered and coated in dark liquid. The wide, hollow white stem grows rapidly over one or two days to give the fruiting body a rather phallic appearance.

Spore production

The dark olive-brown sticky liquid that develops on a white cap contains the spores and is held in place within indentations in the cap surface. The spores are smooth, slim ovals and yellow, although this color is hidden by the overall color of the liquid.

Sensory characteristics

As the name suggests, the stinkhorn reeks of rotting meat. This attracts flies to feed on the spore liquid on its cap surface. Flies then carry the spores stuck on their bodies over long distances. The flies reveal the puckered white cap beneath.

Immature specimens still at the egg stage can be moved and hatched elsewhere if you want to observe the expansion more closely.

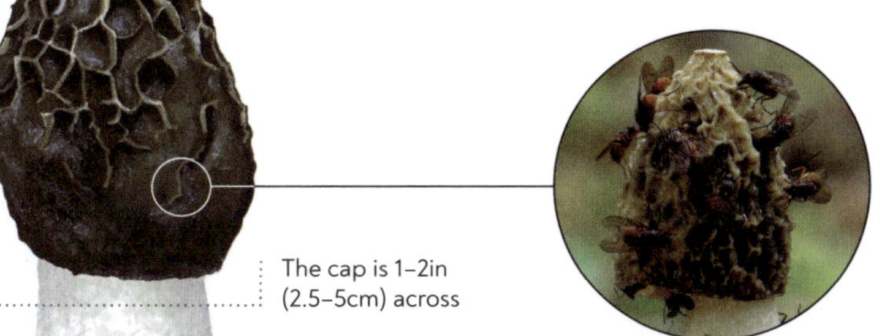

Feeding flies
The dark liquid that coats the cap of the stinkhorn is attractive to flies, who quickly remove it.

MYCORRHIZAE

The mycelia of mycorrhizal fungi dwell underground, intertwining with living plant roots and extending into the soil. The fungi and plants become active, influential partners, giving and receiving materials and signals, with wide-ranging effects on their health and development. Most plants depend on mycorrhizal fungi to survive and thrive.

Types of mycorrhizae
The most common type of mycorrhizae make branching structures inside root cells (endomycorrhizae), which produce spores when the host roots die. Some woody plants associate with fungi that make sheaths around their roots (ectomycorrhizae). Other mycorrhizae associate with ericaceous plants and orchids.

What mycorrhizae do
Mycorrhizae facilitate water, phosphate, and nitrate transport to plants from beyond the reach of their roots and can connect neighboring root systems. The plant gives the fungus its sugars and, in some cases, fatty acids, which it uses as food and to build new cells. While mycorrhizae can help their plant partners, they have their own survival agenda and sometimes take more than they give back.

Effect on plant health
Mycorrhizae enhance plant health by improving their drought tolerance and protecting roots from soil-borne diseases like verticillium wilt. Some mycorrhizae directly interact with pathogens to stop them from entering roots. They can also help plants respond more effectively to resist pathogens' entry and spread. Where fungi connect neighboring root systems, they may even transfer the signaling molecules that protect neighboring plants against attacks.

Partnering up
Mycorrhizal fungi can be highly specialized for a small range of related hosts, or they can be generalists that are not fussy about which plants they join with. For optimal long-term health, plants will form both generalist and specialized associations with fungi, and their partnerships may differ during different life stages.

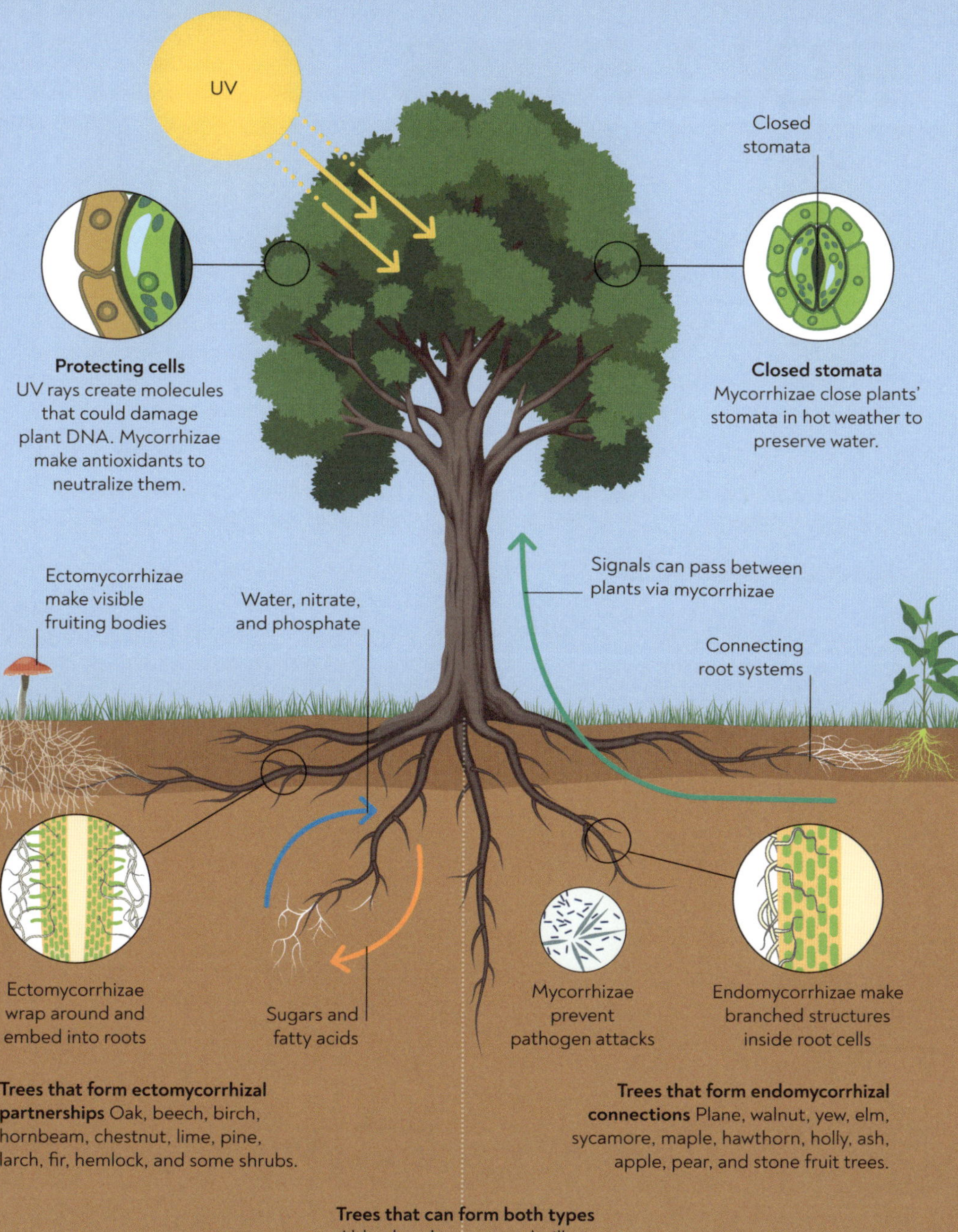

Trees that form ectomycorrhizal partnerships Oak, beech, birch, hornbeam, chestnut, lime, pine, larch, fir, hemlock, and some shrubs.

Trees that form endomycorrhizal connections Plane, walnut, yew, elm, sycamore, maple, hawthorn, holly, ash, apple, pear, and stone fruit trees.

Trees that can form both types
Alder, hazel, aspen, and willow.

ROLLRIMS

Scientific name
Paxillus species, including *P. involutus, P. obscurisporus, P. ammoniavirescens*, and *P. cuprinus*

Distribution Collectively widespread and occasional to common

Habitat Roots of coniferous and deciduous trees

When to see Early summer to late fall

Type Mushroom

Spore production Gills

Spores

Three species of rollrims appear in gardens. They have large caps (*P. involutus* up to 5in/12cm; *P. cuprinus* up to 6in/15cm; *P. ammoniavirescens* up to 8in/20cm; *P. obscurisporus* 12in/30cm) that never fully unroll. Subtle differences in their cap color and texture help distinguish them. *P. involutus* is various shades of brown and covered in matted hairs; *P. cuprinus* starts pale but matures to copper-brown; *P. ammoniavirescens* has brighter shades of brown with flat scales and ribbed edges; and *P. obscurisporus* is reddish-brown.

Their stems match the cap colors and are squat at around $\frac{5}{8}$in (1.5cm) thick for both *P. involutus* and *P. cuprinus*, up to 1in (2.5cm) for *P. ammoniavirescens*, and 1$\frac{1}{4}$in (3cm) for *P. obscurisporus*.

Each species prefers to partner with different trees: *P. involutus* under birch, pine, and spruce; *P. obscurisporus* under oak, lime, and poplar; *P. cuprinus* under birch, alder, and hazel; and *P. ammoniavirescens* under willow, hornbeam, and lime.

Spore production
Tightly packed whitish to yellow-brown gills extend down the stem, producing smooth, oval spores. Spores are olive-brown, or purple-brown for *P. obscurisporus*.

Sensory characteristics
Rollrims have a vaguely pleasant scent and their flesh bruises red-brown when damaged.

Rollrims are mycorrhizal on different trees according to species.

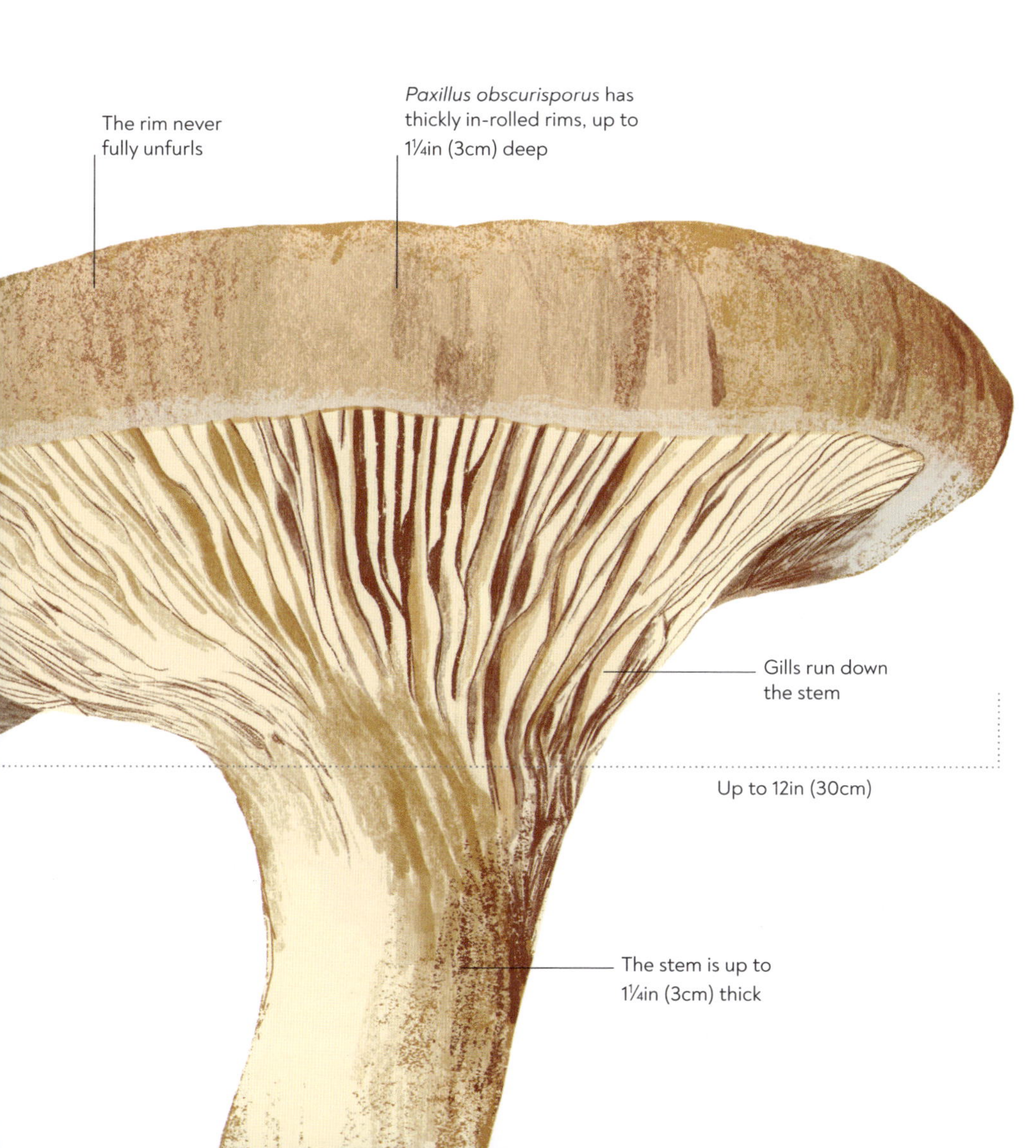

The rim never
fully unfurls
Paxillus obscurisporus has
thickly in-rolled rims, up to
1¼in (3cm) deep
Gills run down
the stem
Up to 12in (30cm)
The stem is up to
1¼in (3cm) thick

POTATO EARTHBALL

Scientific name
Scleroderma bovista

Distribution Widespread and common across most temperate latitudes and occasional in tropical latitudes

Habitat With roots of broadleaved trees

When to see Midsummer to late fall

Type Stomach

Spore production Sac

Spores

These understated brown balls often have a flattened top and appear in groups at the edges of paths. Their thin, pale skin is covered in flat brown scales and is gathered at the base to form a rudimentary stem connecting to white, rootlike strands. The common earthball (*S. citrinum*) differs as its skin is thicker, more coarsely scaly, has no stem nub, and prefers acidic soil.

Spore production
The internal tissue goes from white to black with white marbling to finally form black, powdery spores. The spores are released when the skin ruptures and are round and covered with a net of spiky fins.

Sensory characteristics
The skin of the potato earthball bruises red when damaged and smells like rubber.

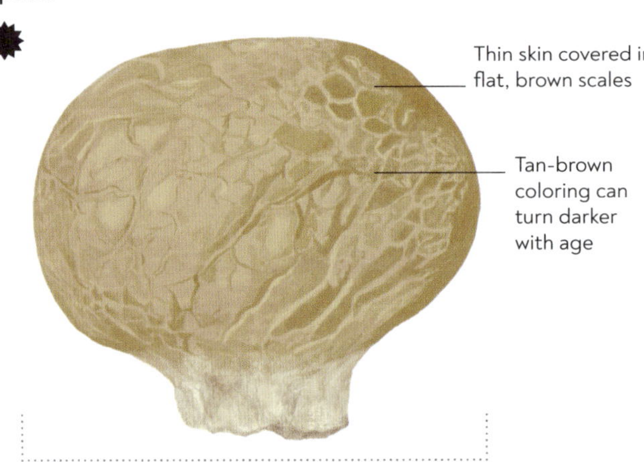

Dark spores
The inside changes from white to black and is filled with powdery spores.

BROWN BIRCH BOLETE

Scientific name
Leccinum scabrum

Distribution Widespread in Europe and North America, including the far north. Introduced and increasing in Australia and New Zealand

Habitat Birch tree roots in dry, acidic soils

When to see Midsummer to midfall

Type Mushroom

Spore production Pores

Spores

Found in dry and acidic soil with birch trees, these mushrooms have deeply domed caps in variable shades of brown that crack up with age. Their tall, thick stems are white and covered with raised black flecks; both the stem and the flecks are thickest at the base.

Spore production
Beneath the cap are spongy, cream pores, which may or may not join the stem. From there, brown, smooth, or spindle-shaped spores are dropped.

Sensory characteristics
The dry cap feels soft but becomes sticky when wet. When bruised, the pores turn brown and the white inner flesh sometimes turns reddish-pink. Edible when cooked.

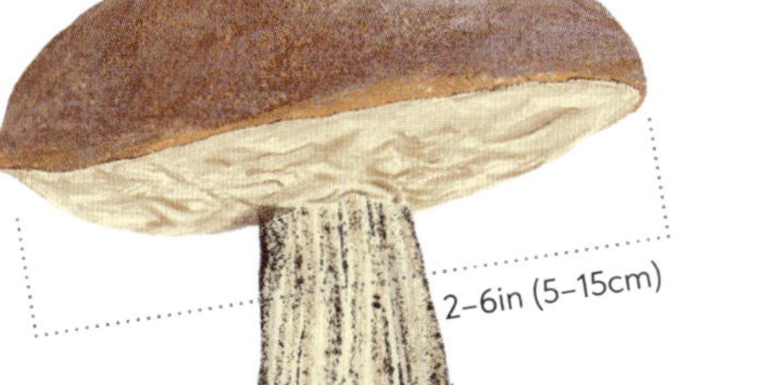

PATHOGENS

Pathogens are distinct from most garden fungi in that they harm live plant tissues. They gain access to their hosts by releasing molecules that silence alarm signals or disable plant defense mechanisms, allowing them to damage the host.

While some pathogens, such as honey fungus (*Armillaria mellea*), can kill a long list of plants, most cause limited damage. Moderate outbreaks of leaf spots, powdery mildews, rusts, and smuts can be tolerated and managed. Removing infected material or thickly mulching to trap last season's spores will interrupt a pathogen's life cycle and slow its spread. Well-planned planting schemes, care routines, and building healthy microbiomes for plants and soil can suppress infection and empower plants to defend themselves against attacks.

Preventing disease issues

Stressed plants are easily infected by pathogens, so choose plants that suit your garden conditions and care for them by planting correctly, regularly mulching woody plants without crowding the stem, irrigating, and pruning as appropriate so they are in excellent general health. Plants have different levels of resistance against diseases, so select plants that can cope with the pathogens you are most concerned about. Find information about cultivar resistance on growers' websites or search for specific diseases to find lists ranking the resistance of plants against major diseases.

OPPOSITE BELOW Ornate galls of pear rust (*Gymnosporangium sabinae*).

OPPOSITE RIGHT Cucurbit powdery mildew (various *Erysiphales* species).

LEFT Honey fungus (*Armillaria mellea*) mycelium fans under bark.

ABOVE Yucca leaf spot (*Coniothyrium concentricum*).

Managing honey fungus

Honey fungus root rot is the most common killer of garden plants. Infected plants can die suddenly as though hit by severe drought, but cutting away the bark at the root crown reveals the telltale white sheets of honey fungus mycelium. The fungus feeds on the dead roots and will spread to neighboring plants unless infected stumps and major roots are promptly removed. When digging out infected roots, do not damage other plants, as wounds are open doors for the fungus. Burn or dispose of the waste (do not compost it). Leave the patch fallow for a year and cultivate the ground to disrupt fungal regrowth, then replant with more resistant plants that suit the site. Adding biochar to planting holes may have some benefits, but no commercial biological controls have been shown to protect roots from honey fungus, and may even make the disease worse.

Surviving plants can deploy root defenses to slow or stop the infection progress, so treat them well to help them mount their best defense. For specimen plants with the root rot, contractors can extend their lifespan by using a compressed jet of air (an "air-spade") to clear the root collar of soil, making it harder for the fungus to girdle the stem and kill the plant.

HONEY FUNGUS

Scientific name
Armillaria mellea

Distribution Widespread and common in the northern hemisphere

Habitat Roots of a wide range of plants

When to see Late fall on living and dead plants

Type Mushroom

Spore production Gills

Spores

This fungus has large clumps of mushrooms 2¾–5in (7–13cm) tall, colored honey-beige on the cap and stem but darkening with age. Renowned as the cause of honey fungus root rot disease, the roots and lower trunk of infected trees and shrubs develop flat white sheets of mycelium under their bark, which spreads to neighboring plants by root-to-root contact. Long, thick cords (rhizomorphs) made of a pale center inside a brittle, brown-black coating search for new hosts or food.

Spore production
White, crowded gills attached to the stem drop white spores, often visible on low-down caps, which are smooth-walled, chubby ovals.

Sensory characteristics
Its mycelial sheets smell mushroomy and its mushrooms smell savory when young. The mushrooms are even edible when properly prepared. Bootlaces (rhizomorphs) can be distinguished from roots as they will snap readily when pulled apart and float in water (most roots sink).

Armillaria gallica
A. gallica can harm only plants that are already weak or stressed. If your honey fungus is *A. gallica*, you'll see plenty of strong rhizomorphs in the soil (those of *A. mellea* are few and fragile), and the mushrooms have a swollen stem (their common name is the bulbous honey fungus).

2–5in (5–13cm)
Cap variation
The color of the mushroom caps ranges from yellow to brown.
Tightly packed white gills
A white-yellow membranous ring sits high on the stem
Dark flecks gather at the center of the cap

SILVERLEAF FUNGUS

Scientific name
Chondrostereum purpureum

Distribution Widespread and common everywhere

Habitat Deciduous trees, particularly stone fruit, apple, and pear trees

When to see Fall to winter

Type Polypore

Spore production
On its lower surface

Spores

Wavy purple plaques grow flush against tree bark then develop pale, fuzzy top rims and can appear in large numbers.

Spore production
Underneath the frilly brackets remains purple and smooth and forms the spores, which are white, smooth, and capsule-shaped. Trees become infected when spores enter pruning wounds, so prune host trees during dry weather in summer when wounds can heal quickly and spore production should be low.

Sensory characteristics
Silverleaf disease causes leaves to turn silver. This happens because the leaf tissues separate due to a toxin released by the fungus that travels up the wood, darkly staining the sapwood as it goes.

Distinctive color
The fungus has a leathery appearance and is purple-lilac in color.

CUSHION BRACKET

Scientific name
Phellinus pomaceus

Distribution Widespread and frequent at temperate latitudes

Habitat *Prunus* trees

When to see All year

Type Polypore

Spore production
Pores

Spores

This perennial polypore emerges as peachy-brown mounds, becoming larger and more hoof-shaped over many years. Sometimes neighboring fruiting bodies merge together into a longer oval. The reddish-brown internal flesh has horizontal zones for each year of new growth. Its mycelium causes a white rot in pruning wounds but can also break down the living sapwood of stressed trees, worsening their health even more.

Spore production
The off-white lower surface is covered with minute hairs and pricked with four to nine pores per millimeter. The spores are cream and smooth but thick-walled and shaped like slightly squashed spheres.

Sensory characteristics
The top and sides harden as they age, eventually becoming smooth and woody.

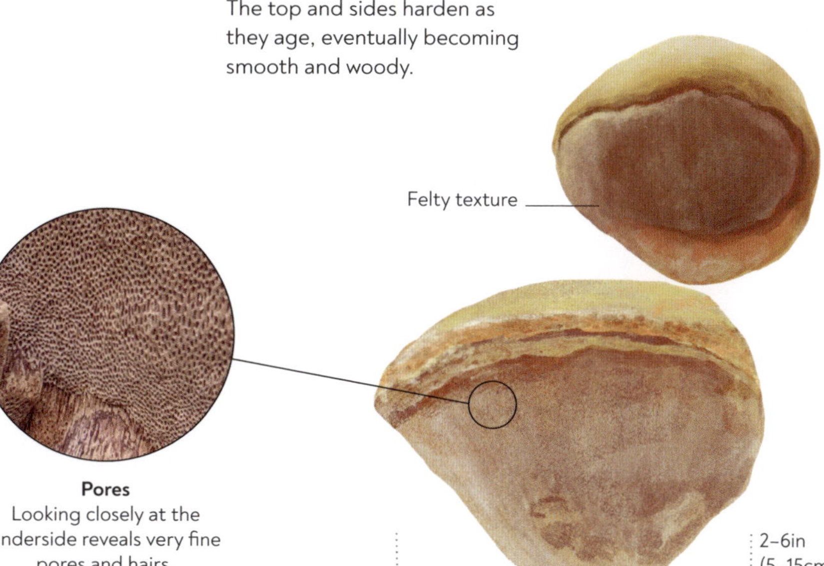

Pores
Looking closely at the underside reveals very fine pores and hairs.

Creating a fungi garden

WHY CREATE A FUNGI GARDEN?

Gardening practices often fail to capitalize on the benefits that fungi can offer. But gardening in fungi-friendly ways can bring out the best in a garden, whatever the style or planting scheme. If you want to successfully create your own fungi garden, you'll need to consider the places that fungi grow, and ways that you can support them.

How fungi help gardeners

The main ways fungi help gardens and gardeners are:

- Recycling dead material
- Partnering with plant roots
- Creating healthy soils
- Enhancing plant health
- Increasing biodiversity
- Forming beautiful and intriguing fruiting bodies
- Producing edible and medicinal fruiting bodies

Sustainable and climate-friendly

Gardens are not often designed to be self-sustaining, and so without the continual addition of various amendments like fertilizers, the vigor of the plants declines. Having a garden rich in fungi greatly reduces or eliminates reliance on these products. Creating landscaping features from natural materials to support fungi also reduces the carbon footprint of a design. These will require periodic maintenance and renewal but buffer gardens from the stresses of extreme heat and waterlogging, and make them more robust against future climate conditions.

Good for body and mind

Growing fungi for harvest is a new challenge for most gardeners. Familiarizing yourself with the way

Creating a fungi garden involves being mindful of the places that fungi occupy.

Heralds of health Fruiting bodies in the garden – like these trooping funnels (*Infundibulicybe geotropa*) – are a sign of a healthy fungal network below ground.

mycelium swells and differentiates is itself enriching, plus the nutrition and culinary appeal of fungi make ideal companions to plant-based produce. Studying the fungi that fruit in your space is excellent for mental health, as focusing on minute and unfamiliar details forces us to slow down and challenge our assumptions.

Ecosystems and conservation

Encouraging fungi in our gardens drives the development of more stable and biodiverse ecosystems. It helps join up corridors of wild fungi to assist in their survival and conservation, plus fungal habitats benefit pollinating insects, supporting plant productivity and conservation of these declining garden visitors. Recording wild fruiting fungi from your garden in biological databases supports conservation efforts, too, helping scientists track the impacts of climate change on fungal abundance and behaviors.

ENCOURAGING HEALTHY SOIL

Fungi in the garden mostly dwell in the soil, so the starting point for creating a fungi garden is to treat soils sensitively. There are bustling communities of invisible life in soil that can do much of the work that gardeners try to do themselves.

Dig sparingly

Instead of digging over soils, let fungal mycelia do this work for you. As hyphae extend through the soil, they improve soil structure by binding particles and introducing air spaces between them. Mycelium is easily broken up by physical disturbance like digging, turning, and sieving, so try to unearth only enough space for planting holes. Fungal communities can tolerate infrequent, mild soil disturbance, and degraded soils can benefit from it as it allows wild spores to embed into them.

Use what you grow

Removing leaf litter and prunings from gardens strips them of the nutritional and microbial cycling that drives long-term, sustainable resilience. Furthermore, it costs gardeners in money (which is spent on products making up for the nutritional shortfall) and in time and effort (which is spent on waste removal). Reusing dead plant material in the garden feeds the fungi, which feed the plants.

Mulch

Soil recycler fungi can be fed without the need to dig in soil improvers, which preserves mycelial connections. Adding plant-based mulch made from leaves, grass clippings, or woodchips to the soil surface will feed decomposer fungi. Varying the plant materials used will increase the range of fungi that contribute to this. Mulches, and the fungi that transform them into humus, improve the nutrition of soil and dampen fluctuations in water availability and temperature. They also suppress plants in unwelcome places when laid thickly. Garden waste can also be used to make your own compost (see pp101–102) to mulch and improve soil.

Fertilizers

Synthetic NPK fertilizers (containing nitrogen, phosphorus, and potassium) make plants dependent on these inputs to grow well, which deters them from forming mycorrhizal connections (see pp78–79). When nutrients are freely available, there is no incentive to enter into the

ABOVE LEFT Avoid frequent digging, which damages mycelia.

ABOVE RIGHT Chip woody waste to make mulch.

BELOW Top-dress beds with homemade compost.

When annual bedding plants die back, their mycorrhizal roots turn into spore factories.

partnership where plants have to expend sugar and fat resources to satisfy the fungal partner, despite this being a very affordable cost to the plant and one they have evolved to pay. Mycorrhizae supply plants with nutrition for a lifetime, and the partnership provides added benefits like protection against pathogens and drought.

Mycorrhizal products

Spend time sensitively nurturing your garden, and your plants will naturally form mycorrhizal associations with local, wild fungi that are already abundant in garden soils. Unlike wild fungi, the spores packaged in mycorrhizal products are not adapted to your local conditions, and the viability of the spores within them varies greatly depending on how they have been stored and transported in the retail chain. Adding fungi on a wide scale that represent a narrow range of genetic diversity can also have negative environmental side effects when the fungi escape into new environments and displace wild fungi in wild places.

Generalist species in mycorrhizal products may be a worse fit for your plants and may be a barrier to better, specialist partnerships that form naturally over time. With each passing year, the fungi that were the most successful partners will grow a bigger population.

Fungicides

Fungicides for use against plant diseases never target only the problematic fungi. We do not have names for most of the fungi that exist, so the full extent of the unintended harm done to other fungi cannot be known. The same can be said for homemade remedies that are often untested and use ingredients like garlic or baking soda. Soil fumigants decimate whole fungal communities; no garden problem is worth the damage they can cause.

OPPOSITE Common earthball (*Scleroderma citrinum*) spores are common in nature and in commercial mycorrhizal products.

CREATING HABITAT FOR FUNGI

There are several ways to make your garden a space that's fungi-friendly. You could make compost or leaf mold, cultivate fungi, or make soils more hospitable for fungi by adding mulch or "chopping and dropping" pruned material. Leaving soil and dead wood undisturbed also allows fungi to flourish.

Work with nature

Gardeners can find inspiration from woodlands as examples of rich fungal habitats. Woodland soil is disturbed far less often than that in gardens, and more of the plant debris is allowed to remain there, so its nutrients and microbes are recycled back into the ecosystem instead of being cleaned up and removed. Decay fungi help finish off ailing plants to make the space and nutrients available for others.

Wild fungi will fruit in the garden as long as there is plenty of food and moisture, and minimal disturbance.

Building habitat for fungi

Build habitats that will not be disturbed too often to give mycelium time to establish and accumulate resources. Create shade and shelter to protect fungal substrates from UV damage and drying out.

Boost plant health and suppress weeds in a fungi-friendly way by mulching woody plants with woodchips made from hedge trimmings or top-dressing annual beds with compost or leaf mold. Woodchips also make ideal pathways as they resist compaction.

Leave out dead wood in varied species and sizes to support a vibrant community of wood decay fungi. Design ideas include stacking

OPPOSITE Sulphur tuft (*Hypholoma fasciculare*) emerging through woodchip mulch.

Dead and hollow trees are jewels in the crown of a fungi garden.

wood into log piles, arranging cut branches as bed, path, or pond edges, building dead hedges, fashioning natural seating from stumps, or displaying impressive pieces as natural works of art. Wood without bark can be eye-catching and enigmatic, although it is drier and fewer fungi can survive there. Dead and hollow trees are the most valuable of all woody habitats and should be prized in the garden.

Making leaf mold

Making leaf mold is an easy job that harnesses the beneficial processes driven by fungi to improve garden soils. Collecting fallen leaves and adding them to a staked chicken wire pen will produce leaf mold in two years that makes a great seed sowing compost or component of potting mix. If you make leaf mold from a wide range of plants, it will contribute to a richer microbiome that includes fungi with a range of diets: unfussy generalists or specialized picky eaters.

Welcome wild fungi

Spores travel on wind, rain, wildlife, boots, seeds, and plants, so you don't need to add them yourself to encourage more fungi in a garden. Over time, fungi will arrive naturally and compete for space and resources. Spontaneously occurring communities will feature the species that are best adapted to the flora and conditions of the site.

Cultivating fungi

Gardeners might be motivated to grow fruiting bodies for their beauty and sensory appeal among a planting design, to harvest the produce for food or medicines, or to support wildlife in the garden.

There are a number of possible combinations of substrates and fungal species to experiment with. Different fungi prefer particular substrates, ranging from cut logs, woodchips, or spawn blocks made of more refined materials like straw, sawdust, cereal bran, soy hulls, coir, cardboard, or coffee grounds.

Whether or not your project flushes with fruiting bodies, it will provide decaying organic matter that supports plant and soil health. For the best fruiting body production, position your designs where they will maintain moist conditions in indirect light. Fungi logs and woodchip spawn instantly look at home in gardens, so consider placing them in interesting patterns or at varying heights, for instance, as upright pillars or used to build raised beds.

Any places where woodchips are laid down can double as productive fungi growing spaces, but woodchip spawn beds also work as stand-alone features. Spawn blocks formed in grow bags can be buried in trenches or kept in their bags and placed or hung on tree branches, bird tables, and fences. Blend grow bags into your garden theme by styling them with macramé hangers, burlap cloaks, woven willow cages, or more inventive materials.

Make your own compost

Composting enables you to reuse garden waste by combining a balance of green (leafy/lush) and brown (woody/dry/spent fungal

TOP LEFT Collect healthy fallen leaves to make leaf mold.

ABOVE Style grow kits with macramé hangers.

ABOVE LEFT Piling up logs helps them stay damp, creating suitable conditions for fungi.

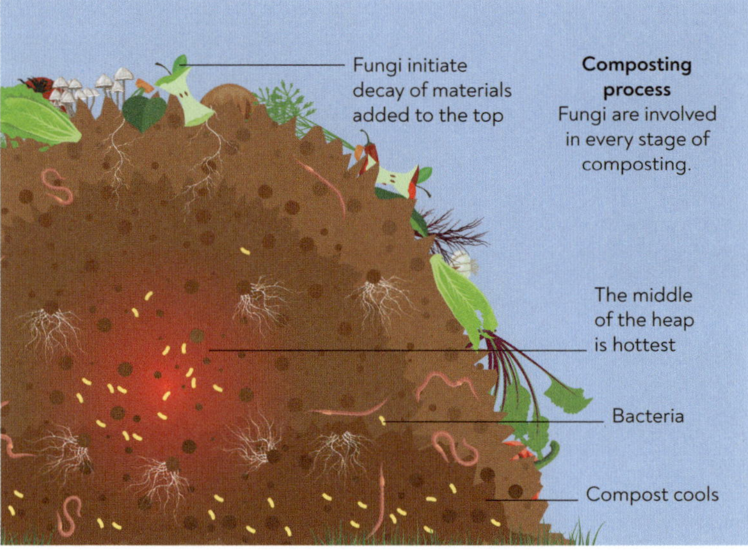

substrates) shredded material. Ensure the mix is damp but not wet (either by watering or keeping out rain). Turn the compost from time to time to mix in fresh oxygen to speed up its decomposition by fungi, bacteria, and invertebrates.

Three phases occur in the making of compost, and fungi are crucial in all of them: readily accessible compounds are broken down, which generates heat; then heat-loving microorganisms break down complex plant polymers; then decay slows and the compost cools and matures.

Except for hot composting, don't add diseased plants to your compost, as pathogens are likely to survive. No composting method will kill pathogens in wood and thick roots, so it is best to burn them and then add the ashes to the compost.

Signs of fungi in compost

Fruiting bodies are a good sign that fungi are decaying the brown components in the mixture, although compost with a high proportion of brown contents decomposes more slowly. Sometimes white mycelium is visible, or thicker white fungal cords, and both are welcome signs | of helpful fungal decay. If you find dry, black bootlaces (rhizomorphs), they are a sign that honey fungus (see pp86–87) has got in, but finding lots of them points to it being the less destructive species (*Armillaria gallica*). To be on the safe side, avoid using compost with honey fungus rhizomorphs in it.

Compost tea

Steeping compost in water to produce compost tea has a popular following, but the claims

The spent substrate of native fungi grow kits can be composted, counting as a brown ingredient.

that compost tea can combat diseases or nourish soils are unsupported by evidence. The concept of creating a brew of locally adapted antagonistic microbes to suppress plant pathogens has merit but is not a likely outcome as every batch made is different. In the unlikely event that a compost tea was made containing high nutrient levels for use as a quick-release fertilizer, using it would harm a fungi garden by weakening plant-mycorrhizal relationships.

Spent mushroom substrates

The waste from supermarket mushroom (*Agaricus bisporus*) production is sold as a cheap soil conditioner. It is often made from composted straw, chalk, and the farmed fungal mycelium but may also contain peat and isn't as beneficial for your garden as homemade compost.

The spent substrates from fruiting body grow kits of native fungi, such as oyster mushrooms (*Pleurotus ostreatus*), can be composted, counting as brown ingredients. Avoid adding spent substrate from nonnative grow kits to gardens, unless you are able to denature the mycelium within it, for instance by pressure-cooking, to prevent any potentially invasive cultivated exotic species from escaping into the wild.

RIGHT The rate that fungi, bacteria, and invertebrates convert garden and kitchen waste into compost varies with the setup used. A cold composting bin, shown here, will take longer than hot composting.

EDIBLES AND OUTDOOR GROWING

Cultivating fungi outdoors is less reliable than using a good setup indoors, as outdoors is more prone to fluctuations in humidity, temperature, sunlight exposure, contaminants, and to grazing wildlife. It may take some trial and error to find the ideal position for different types of fungal spawn in the garden. But regardless of how well they fruit, adding substrates (such as woodchip or fresh logs) inoculated with native decay fungi, will enhance a garden's soil health, plant health, and biodiversity status.

Native strains

Fungi growers often sell and promote nonnative strains, but it is irresponsible to use them outdoors. Cultivated species are selected for vigorous fruiting, which helps them spread beyond the cultivated area. When species invade wild spaces and outcompete native fungi, it causes ecological harm, as with the golden oyster in North America (see p29).

In the absence of formal regulations, it falls to fungi growers themselves to engage in ecologically responsible practices that protect native fungal diversity. Fungi gardeners can apply pressure on the market to increase the range of native strains available by asking growers to share strains' provenance and purchasing native fungi only for outdoor use.

Protected species

The few fungal species that have been given protected status due to their extinction risk are illegal to pick, destroy, or sell. This causes an ethical dilemma for those in the UK wishing to cultivate the protected lion's mane outdoors. As growers must rely on nonnative strains, there is a risk that these will escape into the wild and hybridize with native strains or outcompete the native population, accelerating its extinction.

Identifying species

Always check that emerging fruiting bodies matches the strains you intended to grow as wild spores will land on and may be capable of taking over the substrates of your cultivation projects. Never consume fungi unless you are certain of their identity, which is not often easy as color, shape, and size can be variable, and reference descriptions are often difficult to interpret without the assistance of a more knowledgeable guide.

ABOVE RIGHT Oyster mushrooms (*Pleurotus ostreatus*) grown outdoors must be kept moist to obtain good yields.

RIGHT Fruiting bodies attract wildlife, like the larvae inside these oysterlings (*Crepidotus* sp.).

FUNGI GROW BAGS

The simplest way to begin cultivating fungi at home is to use a premade grow bag kit. Each kit has its own instructions to reach a harvest and involve making a small cut in the grow bag and misting the mycelium regularly for around two weeks. Practicing with growing kits indoors may better prepare you for outdoor growing. Choose your kit carefully, as the quality of the mycelium and sustainability of the materials used varies. After the first flush of mushrooms, good-quality kits can produce a second or third crop.

Why cultivate fungi?

People usually grow mushrooms to consume them as food or health supplements. However, it is also worth growing fungal fruiting bodies for their inherent beauty or ecological benefits (see pp92–93). The oyster mushroom (*Pleurotus ostreatus*) and dryad's saddle (*Cerioporus squamosus*) are two native, edible species of cultivated fungi that work well in grow bags. If harvesting to eat, twist off mushrooms when they reach their peak (fully expanded but before the caps begin to wither), and keep on misting for a few more weeks to obtain a second or even third flush.

Keep it local

While there are many different strains and species of mushroom kits sold, only a minority are sourced from your local habitat. A successful outdoor flush of mushrooms will release billions of spores into the wild and using nonnative species or strains threatens local fungi that are already struggling against habitat fragmentation. To prevent distant

The oyster mushroom is a fast-growing species that is one of the most widely cultivated fungi in the world.

Native spawn
Check with suppliers which native strains they stock. They are likely to have native oyster mushrooms (*Pleurotus ostreatus*).

relatives from replacing local fungal diversity, it is crucial to select strains for outdoor use that are from as close to home as possible (see p139).

Find a good spot

Once you've sourced your kit, you'll need to find it a suitable place in the garden. Choose somewhere cool and mostly shaded to protect it from drying out too quickly. Hanging it or placing it off the ground will also prevent it from sitting in pooled water and deter ground-dwelling insects from grazing on or inhabiting your fungus. The grow bag can be cloaked in a burlap sack or hung in a macramé hanger to improve its appearance before the mushrooms become visible and steal the show.

HOW TO MAKE YOUR OWN GROW BAGS

Fungal spawn suppliers sell the materials to prepare your own grow bags. Doing so will save you money and enable you to experiment with different species and strains beyond what is available in kits.

WHAT YOU NEED

- 5oz (150g) straw pellets
- Sterile plastic bag with filter patch
- Boiled water
- Local mushroom grain spawn (e.g., rye with oyster mycelium)
- Tape or heat sealer
- Clean hands and worktops

1 **Prepare the substrate**
Working indoors somewhere clean with little air movement, add the straw pellets to the sterile plastic bag and pour over boiled water until the straw cannot absorb more. Agitate the pellets through the bag to ensure they have all broken up and there are no dry spots. If water pools in the bag, you have added too much and will have to start again.

2 **Add the mycelium spawn**
Squeeze the grain spawn to loosen it from its block while it's in the bag. Working swiftly to prevent contamination, cut the bag open and pour some of the grain spawn out to cover the layer of straw. Keeping plenty of air in the top of the bag containing the straw, roll the end over and tape it shut or use a heat sealer, then shake the straw and grain to get an even mixture. The filter in the bag will allow the mycelium to receive clean air.

3 **Incubate**
Place the bag indoors somewhere dark that will stay at a stable room temperature. Check on it every few days for increasing white mycelium growth and to ensure no dark or slimy contamination is visible. After 2–4 weeks, the mycelium should have colonized the straw, creating a rigid block.

1

2

3

4

4 **Grow fruiting bodies**
Position the grow bag in the garden in a shady spot off the ground. Make two cuts forming a cross about 4in (10cm) wide in the lower center of the bag. Mist the opening every other day with fresh water, and once mushroom pins begin to form, increase the rate of misting to twice a day. Different species will have a different peak size for picking, but it is best to harvest before wrinkling begins around the edges by twisting them off. Continue misting in the same pattern to initiate a second or third flush.

Recycle the materials
Native spawn can be crumbled and composted when finished. If mushrooms grow in your heap, identify them carefully, and consume them only if you're sure they are the same species. Clean well and remove the filter patch to recycle the bag with soft plastics.

MAKING FUNGI LOGS

Fungi logs are a fun project to set up and their natural aesthetic can be styled to complement all sorts of garden designs. With minimal upkeep, they will produce fungi for a few years.

Obtaining suitable logs can be a challenge unless you have a lot of trees on site. Only freshly cut logs can be used to cultivate fungi from, as older logs will already be colonized by wild fungi. Wood must be healthy, with the bark intact and free from clear signs of fungal decay, especially pathogenic fungi that would be able to spread into living trees (such as honey fungus and silver leaf, see pp86–88). After cutting, logs should be "seasoned" by waiting for 2–6 weeks after they're cut to allow a small influx of air as fungal activity relies on oxygen.

Placing the logs in your space

Adding fungi logs to a garden can make an attractive feature with year-round appeal as well as a productive space. Stacking logs together somewhere shady and sheltered will help them stay moist during the long incubation period. Combine logs alongside those inoculated with fungi to make any structures bigger and more impactful and ensure fungi logs have enough room to flush with fruiting bodies. A crib stack formation is a good way to arrange fungi logs as it has a small footprint and provides access to each log for easy harvesting. Alternatively, lean logs against a fence, bury one end to stand them upright, make them into the edges of a raised bed or path, or create any arrangement that suits your space.

Pale oyster
The pale oyster is a good choice for cultivating on a log in the garden during warmer months. You can harvest once the caps are fully open.

Food for wildlife
Turkey tails on silver birch logs are grown for their wildlife benefits.

Choosing which fungi to grow
Many types of oysters, such as the pale oyster (*Pleurotus pulmonarius*), suit log growing. Other suitable edibles include the velvet foot (*Flammulina velutipes*) and sheathed woodtuft (*Kuehneromyces mutabilis*) mushrooms and the annual polypore hen of the woods (*Grifola frondosa*).

There is no way to responsibly grow lion's mane on logs outdoors in the UK, as it is illegal to sell native strains. While using nonnative strains is not illegal, it increases the extinction threat to the native fungi populations. Shiitake is another popular nonnative that should be reared indoors for the same reasons.

The rewards of a successful project are long-lived as colonized logs can flush with fruiting bodies for several years.

HOW TO MAKE FUNGI LOGS

Fungi logs provide long-lived grow projects that look impressive and have a high value for garden wildlife.

WHAT YOU NEED

- Seasoned, healthy hardwood logs about 3¼ft (1m) long, 4–8in (10–20cm) thick
- Power drill
- ⅓in (8mm) drill bit for wood
- Native fungi hardwood dowel spawn
- Hammer
- Beeswax pellets
- Double boiler pan
- Thick paintbrush
- Hob/camping stove

1 **Drill holes**
Drill holes into the sides of the logs for individual dowels, ensuring a snug fit of width and depth. Stagger holes with regular spacing to create a diagonal pattern that maximizes the room for each dowel to grow before meeting another mycelium.

2 **Add fungi dowel spawn**
Using one fungal strain per log, hammer a dowel into each hole until it is flush with the bark. Melt the wax in the double boiler pan and paint molten wax onto each hole to seal the dowel inside. Optionally, you can also coat the cut log ends with wax to help retain moisture and reduce access to wild fungi.

3 **Incubate and water**
Incubate the logs in a compact log pile for 6–12 months somewhere shady and sheltered outdoors or in an unheated greenhouse or shed. Keep them off the ground using either a pallet or other logs without fungi in them to protect the fungi logs from soil-borne microbes and wildlife. Monitor the fungi logs for moisture levels by feeling their heaviness. If they seem to be losing water weight, periodically soak them for a few hours in a water barrel of nonchlorinated water, or you can mist with them with tap water for about an hour a week.

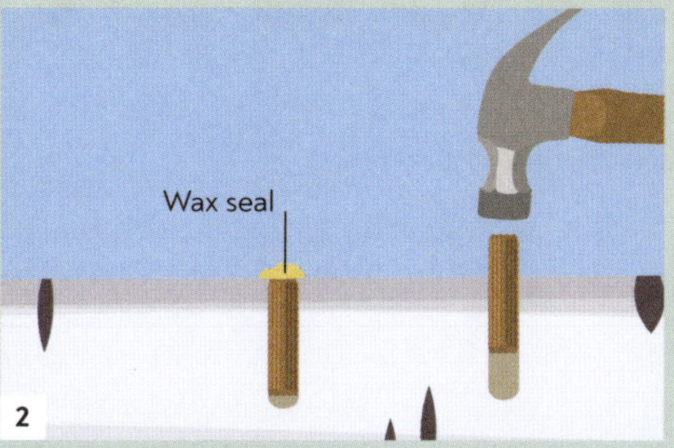

4 Grow fruiting bodies
As fruiting season approaches, rearrange the logs so the sides are exposed to give room for fruiting bodies to emerge. Some species will start fruiting naturally according to environmental cues, but others may need an added "shock," such as a 24-hour long soak in fresh water, or being hit against the ground, each other, or a hammer to initiate fruiting body formation. If harvesting, twist them away at the base when the fruiting bodies are widely expanded.

Repeat and repurpose logs
When the fruiting body flush has finished, pile the logs up again to preserve their moisture for most of the year, then expand the pile during the fruiting period. A well-colonized log and a prolific fungal strain could stay productive for over five years before being used elsewhere in the garden.

GROWING FUNGI ON WOODCHIP

Woodchip is one of the most active habitats for fungi in gardens. Having plenty of chips in your garden—either as pathways, mulch, or fungi beds—will benefit plants, soil, wild fungi, and wildlife. Plus, you can get even more from your mulch by cultivating fungal fruiting bodies on it. Producing your own woodchip spawn takes up more room than other fungi garden projects, but the spawn produced will cover larger areas of the garden.

Be aware that most wild fungi that grow on woodchip in garden environments are not edible species.

Which chips should I use?
Mixed chips of various sizes of source wood (from twigs to logs) and species work best for the biggest range of fungi. For instance, after pruning a mixed hedge or shrub border, you will have the ideal stock to pass through a chipper and create your fungal spawn substrate. If there are leaves in the mix, they do not need to be separated out. Most fungi that you may wish to cultivate prefer a mix of deciduous tree wood rather than conifer, but you can experiment with what you have.

Which fungi can I cultivate?
Edible native fungi that can succeed on woodchip beds include oysters, poplar fieldcaps (*Cyclocybe aegerita*), and wood blewits (*Collybia nuda*). While many fungi that grow on woodchip are not edible, some of those that are (such as wine caps, *Stropharia rugosoannulata*) are not suitable for outdoor growing in Britain, as they've been introduced from elsewhere.

Blewits
These flourish on woodchip beds.

HOW TO MAKE WOODCHIP SPAWN

WHAT YOU NEED

- 2 large food-grade barrels with lids
- Fresh, mixed size and species hardwood chips no more than a few weeks old enough for steps 1 and 5
- Cold fresh water
- Strong netting
- Tarp
- Drill with bits for holes around 2in (5cm)
- Native fungal grain or sawdust spawn (e.g., blewits on sawdust; tarragon oyster on rye)

1 Cold-water pasteurize the substrate

Fill a barrel with woodchip, ideally varied species, and with enough clean, cold fresh water (from a rain barrel or tap) to submerge the chips, add something heavy on top to keep the chips from floating above the water level, if needed. Fit the barrel lid and leave for two weeks, during which time any microbes that rely on oxygen will be killed off.

2 Drain and dry the woodchip

On a warm, dry day (or over several days), wrap a net over the barrel opening and tip it over to drain the water. It may be very heavy, so you may need two or more people. Also consider how to lower it slowly to prevent the barrel from cracking with repeated uses. The water may smell foul, but that is a good sign that the microbial community is changing. Lay the tarp on the ground and spread out the chips on top, allowing them to dry and encouraging any microbes that rely on low oxygen environments to die off.

3 Create a chip and spawn "lasagna"

Drill a ring of large holes approximately 2in (5cm) in diameter around the top and bottom of a barrel and fill it up with alternating layers of pasteurized woodchip and spawn, starting and ending with woodchip at the bottom and top. Build the spawn layers from a mixture of handful-sized pieces and finer crumbs for best results.

4 Incubate

Place the barrel somewhere with a relatively stable temperature that will get some extra warmth from the sun (if in winter) or will not get too much sun and dry out (if in summer). The incubation time will vary from 2–8 weeks depending on the season. It isn't easy to monitor the growth of the mycelium in the barrel, but you can brush the top chips away to spy for white mycelium coming up, showing the spawn is ready.

5 Add chips to the garden

In the areas of your choosing, apply the woodchip spawn by sandwiching it between two layers of fresh chips. When decanting spawn from the barrel, don't disrupt the mycelial structure too much and keep some large chunks intact because they will withstand drying out. For fungi beds, place a layer of water-saturated, ink-free cardboard on top of bare ground before adding alternating layers of fresh and spawn chips to fill the depth. Water spawn chips during dry weather to maximize the fruiting body production.

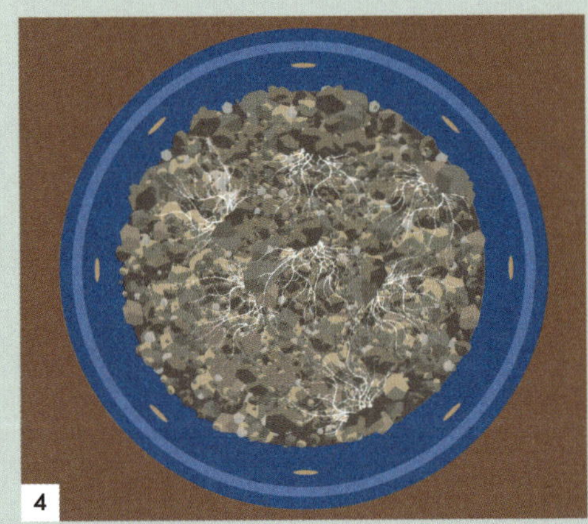

6 Grow fruiting bodies

The time until fruiting varies depending on species and climate. Fungi initiate fruiting seasonally according to environmental cues like day length and temperature, so chip spawn added in spring will often produce fruiting bodies in fall. To harvest, twist off fruiting bodies when caps are wide open but before they wilt and wither. Always check that the fungi species that appear in your woodchip and harvest are the species you chose to grow, as wild, inedible species can appear.

Keep adding woodchip and extra batches of spawn of matching strains each year to boost productivity.

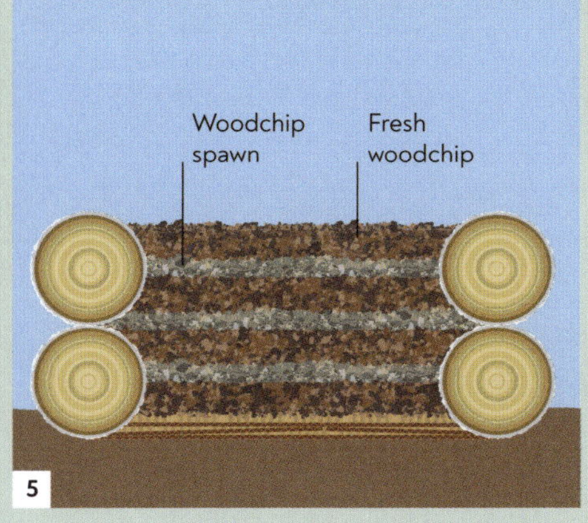

PROPAGATING FUNGI AT HOME

If you want to propagate fungi at home but fungal spawn suppliers do not stock the species or strains that you want to cultivate, it is worth inquiring about their stock, as your request might prompt them to expand their range. If that is not successful, you could propagate them yourself from wild fungi. You could also propagate the fungi from your growing projects.

Growing wild species

You can bring wild fruiting bodies into the garden and let them produce and release spores (sporulate) there. While you may not know whether your attempt has worked for some time, this approach can be effective for prolific spore producers like giant puffballs (see p68), or for vigorous primary colonizers like turkey tail (see pp54–55).

Developing mycelium

The next level up involves growing mycelium from fruiting bodies. This can be done by adding the bases of mushroom stems onto moist cardboard in a simple container. You can also collect spore prints (pp24–25), suspend them in a sterile solution, and then add that to sterilized grain. Grain can be sterilized at home in mason jars with specialized lids using a pressure cooker or bought preprepared.

A more scientific setup for growing mycelium involves cutting and transferring small pieces of internal tissue onto petri dishes filled with agar jelly (a growth medium for microbes that is available ready-made). Restricting the air movement by using a still-air box (a clean, plastic crate with hand holes cut out) and using flame-sterilized tools reduces

If you are collecting wild specimens, never pick protected, rare, vulnerable, or threatened species and pick only from places where you have permission to collect.

the risk of contamination, as agar is an ideal microbial habitat. Petri dishes of fungi are then used to inoculate batches of sterile grain. This method allows you to collect and store fungal cultures in the fridge to regrow onto fresh agar plates when you want them.

Once you have the mycelia of your desired species growing on grain, you can use this to inoculate your unique cultivation projects (see pp106–119).

ABOVE RIGHT Turkey tail (*Trametes versicolor*) spread naturally from fungi logs to this dead hedge.

RIGHT Mycelium from agar spreading onto sterile grain to form grain spawn.

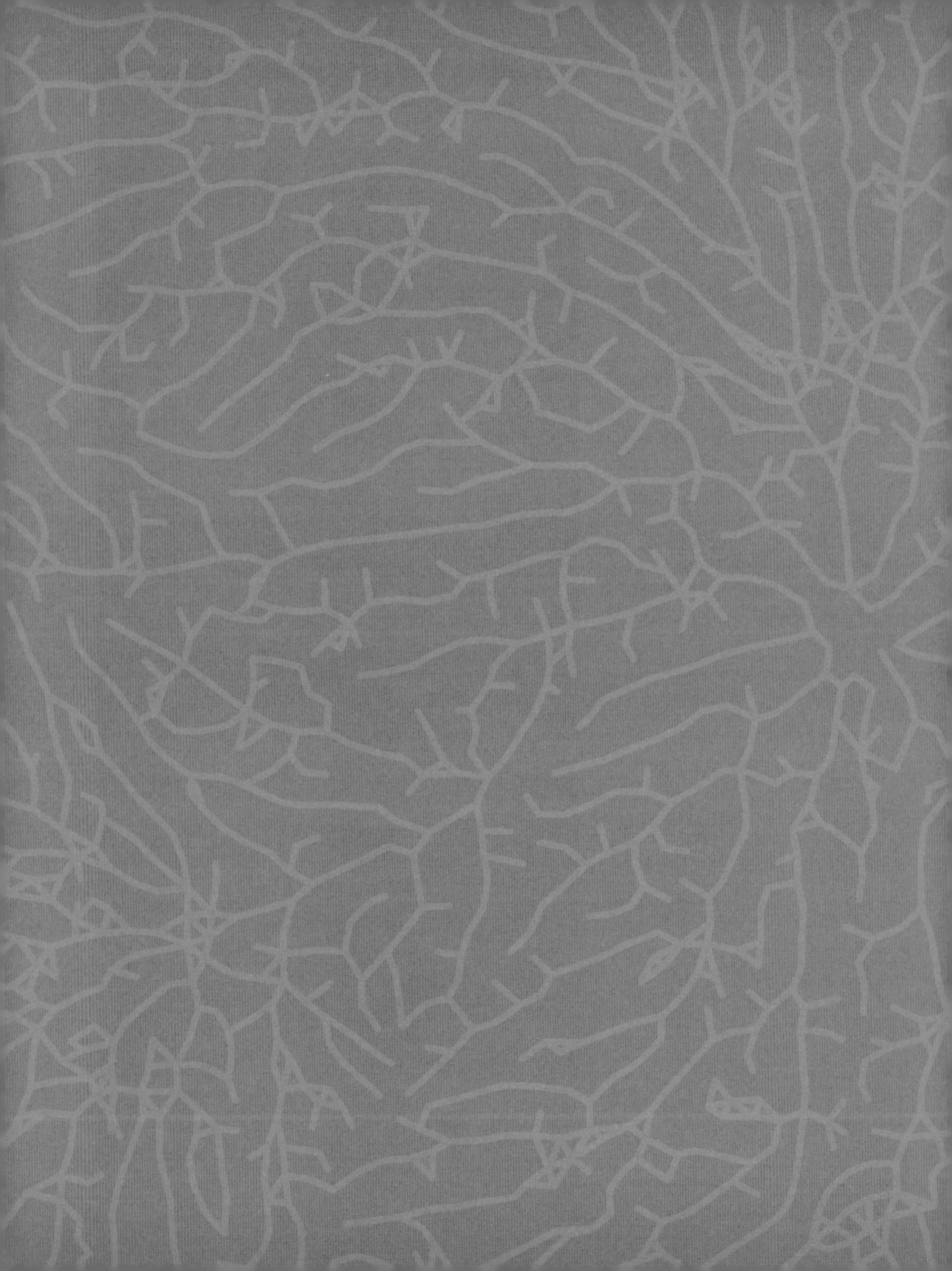

Fungi
garden year

SPRING

Springtime brings longer, warmer days to the garden and new growth of plants and fungi. As the soil warms, the fungi within it grow more rapidly, using any resources obtained during fall and winter to extend the size of their mycelia. Plant growth is resource-intensive, relying on fertile, humus-rich soils created by fungal activity.

New growth, new connections

As plants grow new roots, mycorrhizae gain new tissues to partner with. New shoots and buds present fresh surfaces for airborne fungal spores to germinate on and establish new relationships. In mature and aging trees, as new rings of sapwood form, older rings become heartwood, internalizing the associated fungi.

Annual fruiting bodies

For some fungi, spring is mating season, and so long as there is plentiful rainfall, flushes of annual fruiting bodies will appear. St. George's mushrooms are so named because they appear around the 23rd of April (St. George's Day) and black morels burst up from woodchip mulch. Behind the cherry blossoms, you may spot cushion fungi studded along trunks and branches or halos of fairy ring mushrooms among lush green grass. Even the sulfur tuft, which has historically fruited only in fall, now fruits in spring, with changing climatic conditions thought to be the cause.

Spring offers new chances for plants to grow and fungi to connect.

LEFT Cushion bracket (*Phellinus pomaceus*) on a blossoming *Prunus* tree.

BELOW Black morels (*Morchella importuna*).

BOTTOM RIGHT St. George's mushroom (*Calocybe gambosa*).

BOTTOM LEFT Sulphur tuft (*Hypholoma fasciculare*).

SUMMER

The sunshine and warmth of summer provides ideal growing conditions for plant growth and productivity. This means that for fungi that partner with plants, the nutritional rewards they receive from those plants will be at their peak. They can repay the favor during dry spells, as fungi can reduce drought stress in a number of ways (see pp78–79).

Importance of water

Well-established, climate-appropriate planting schemes, good irrigation, and damp nooks all help support fungi during the summer. Fungal activity and mycelial presence improve water retention in soils and wooden structures, helping plants flourish when rainfall is limited. This is why fungal-colonized logs are ideal to use for raised beds, as they help regulate the moisture level in the compost better than dry logs. Alternatively, if summer thunderstorms bring torrential rainfall, fungi can absorb and transport away excess water and preserve soil structure, mitigating waterlogging and soil erosion.

Drought

Loss of leaves or branches to drought means that endophytic fungi (those that live inside plants) lying in wait as ready recyclers can switch roles and begin the decomposition process. Fungi are less active when dry, but with the return of rainfall, soil-borne decay fungi will redistribute the resources of shed plant parts back into the garden.

Fruiting issues

Given that a fruiting body's mass is often around 90 percent water, hot weather and high UV radiation can create difficult conditions for fungi to fruit. However, some species, such as heartwood fungi, can find enough moisture to fruit through the summer.

Fungi are known to reduce drought stress for plants through a whole suite of mechanisms.

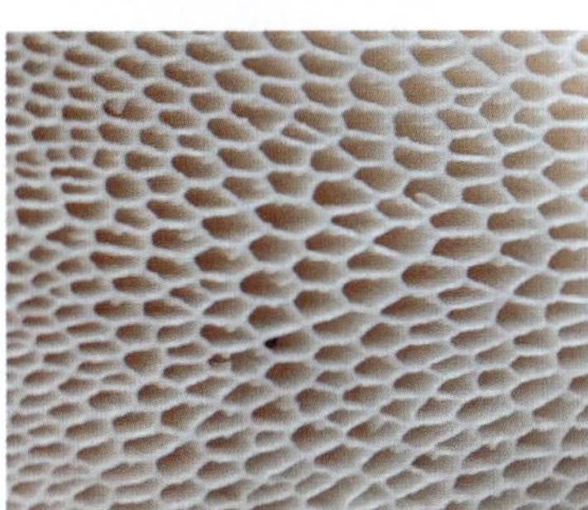

TOP LEFT Chicken of the woods (*Laetiporus sulphureus*) on oak.

TOP RIGHT Shaggy bracket (*Inonotus hispidus*).

CENTER LEFT Wide angular pores of dryad's saddle (*Cerioporus squamosus*).

LEFT Dryad's saddle on a dead trunk.

EARLY FALL

The onset of fall is marked by leaves changing color, seeds ripening, and annual plants dying back. These changes provide ample food sources for recycler fungi that break down dead organic matter. Plants stop defending the tissues they will shed, which weak pathogens like leaf spot fungi (see p84) can take advantage of. As greenery is lost, endophytic fungi inside plants switch into recycler mode.

Showstopper displays

Decay and mycorrhizal fungi will be well resourced to expand their mycelium and compete with their neighbors for territory or invest in reproduction. The cool, humid weather and longer nights of fall are the cues for most species to fruit. Showstopper fungal fruiting bodies can lift your fall garden to new levels of splendor. The display changes rapidly, so immerse yourself in it as much as possible, because the weeks when it is at its peak will quickly pass. Fall is the best time to expand your knowledge by attending forays with local fungus groups. They will have permission to collect specimens that you can take with you to study further or attempt to propagate at home.

Early signs

For those with mature native trees in their garden, ectomycorrhizal fungi (see pp78–79) like the fly agaric (*Amanita muscaria*) might be the ones to announce that fall has arrived. Grassland and woodchip fungi also start fruiting early in the season, some of which will perish all too quickly, like the inkcaps and puffballs (see pp66–68), whereas others like bird's nest fungi (see p37) and earthstars (see p62) will persist for weeks or months.

TOP LEFT Collared earthstar (*Geastrum michelianum*).

TOP RIGHT Fly agaric (*Amanita muscaria*).

CENTER RIGHT Amethyst deceiver (*Laccaria amethystina*).

LEFT Scurfy twiglet (*Tubaria furfuracea*).

MID–LATE FALL

The greatest diversity of fungi fruiting bodies will likely be on show in the garden during midfall. Any early-fruiting species are joined by others that take more convincing that summer has gone, such as rosy bonnets (*Mycena rosea*), wood blewits (*Collybia nuda*), and yellow stainers (*Agaricus xanthodermus*). Honey fungus (*Armillaria* species) mushrooms usually wait until later in the season before appearing.

Fallen leaves

Fungi that live in leaf litter will benefit from fallen leaves so leave them undisturbed, where possible. But clear up any diseased leaves or prunings; otherwise, pathogen populations will increase and their diseases will be worse next year. Some fruiting bodies may become harder to spot as the leaves cover them, so when appreciating a subject, take time to brush away debris to view it more clearly. Likewise, if collecting leaves for leaf mold, gather them gently or risk decapitating the fruiting bodies underneath.

Tree seeds

Fall also sees the ripening and dropping of tree seeds. Specialist fungi are adapted for this unusual niche, and they are well worth keeping an eye out for. Two choice examples are the delightful earpick fungi (*Auriscalpium vulgare*), which emerge between the scales of pine cones, and the tiny orange cups of the hairy nuts disco (*Lanzia echinophila*) that pop up out of sweet chestnut cases or Turkish oak acorns.

When fall is in full swing, fallen leaves gather on the soil and the fungi that live in litter have their heyday.

TOP LEFT Beechleaf bonnets (*Mycena capillaris*).

TOP RIGHT Mica caps (*Coprinellus micaceus*).

CENTER LEFT Rosy bonnets (*Mycena rosea*).

LEFT Trooping funnels (*Infundibulicybe geotropa*).

WINTER

Cold temperatures slow fungal growth and metabolism, and fungi become dormant in winter soils. Many species that spend the summer in green plant tissues cannot tolerate the cold, so they overwinter as thick-walled spores or mycelial lumps (sclerotia).

Below freezing

Swelling ice crystals can rupture cell membranes and walls, but fungi often possess cellular contents that act as antifreeze. The master of ice-manipulation is *Exidiopsis effusa*, a jelly fungus found on dead wood. Compounds released during wood decay restrict the size of ice crystals causing them to assemble into fine chains and create the exquisite phenomenon of "hair ice."

Bringing color

Fluctuating air temperatures present difficult conditions for fleshy fruiting bodies, but several species can withstand cold/thaw cycles and flourish all winter long. Annual fruiting bodies bring flashes of color on gray days then gradually degrade. Crusts paint over cracking bark. Marmalade-orange velvet foot caps (*Flammulina velutipes*) gleam atop clusters of furry, sable-colored stems. Grand trooping funnels (*Infundibulicybe geotropa*) defy the shrinking cold, standing tall above the leaf litter. With fewer invertebrates hunting for a fungal meal and slower microbial activity, the annual fruiting bodies that survive in winter persist for long spells.

Fungi on bare trees

When trees are bare, fruiting bodies on trunks and branches are easier to see. Perennial fruiting bodies cast novel silhouettes. Each year, a new coal-black layer forms around King Alfred's cakes (*Daldinia concentrica*) that conceals shimmering silver rings inside.

Translucent jellies and primary-colored cups gleam in gloomy corners.

LEFT Jelly ears (*Auricularia auricula-judae*).

BELOW Trooping funnel (*Infundibulicybe geotropa*).

CENTER Velvet foot (*Flammulina velutipes*).

BOTTOM LEFT Turkey tail (*Trametes versicolor*).

FUNGI GARDEN CALENDAR

SEASON	ACTIONS FOR GROW BAGS AND PROPAGATING FUNGI	ACTIONS FOR FUNGI LOGS	ACTIONS FOR WOODCHIP SPAWN
Mid–late winter	• Collect and propagate winter species.	• Cut and season fresh logs. • Drill seasoned logs and add fungi dowels. • Move fungi logs to a shed or unheated greenhouse for warmth.	• Pasteurize fresh woodchips. • Layer pasteurized woodchip and grain spawn in barrels. • Incubate barrels in a warm spot for 2–4 weeks.
Early–midspring	• Fruit grow bags of cool-weather species. • Collect and propagate spring species.	• Move fungi logs outdoors. • Stack newly made logs off the ground to prevent competition.	• Lay woodchip spawn as mulch or beds. • Feed existing woodchip beds with fresh woodchip.
Late spring–midsummer	• Fruit grow bags of warm-weather species. • Collect and propagate summer species.	• Cover fungi logs with shade netting to preserve moisture.	• Water woodchip fungi beds if dry.
Late summer–midfall	• Fruit grow bags of cool-weather species. • Collect and propagate fall species.	• Uncover and arrange covered logs ready for fruiting. • Harvest fruiting bodies from fungi logs.	• Harvest woodchip fungi fruiting bodies.
Late fall–early winter	• Fruit grow bags of cool-weather species. • Collect and propagate fall species.	• Cut and season fresh logs. • Drill seasoned logs and add fungi dowels. • Move fungi logs to a shed or unheated greenhouse for warmth.	• Harvest woodchip fungi fruiting bodies.

ACTIONS FOR THE GARDEN	**FEATURED EDIBLE SPECIES**
• Prune woody plants. • Build dead hedges. • Create willow or hazel weavings. • Chip woody waste. • Mulch woody plants with woodchip. • Create or add to woodchip paths.	• Jelly ear • Oyster mushroom • Velvet foot 
• Mow lawn and compost the cuttings. • Start of seedlings in leaf mold. • Top-dress annual beds with compost.	• Morels • Fairy ring mushroom • St. George's mushroom 
• Mow lawns infrequently and compost the cuttings. • Turn compost heap. • Prune *Prunus* trees during dry spells.	• Dryad's saddle • Chicken of the woods • Fairy ring mushroom • Pale oyster
• Keep brown annual stems or chop and drop. • Inspect for disease, prune out, and clean up diseased material. • Burn diseased material and add ashes to compost. • Mow lawns infrequently and compost the cuttings.	• Brown birch bolete • Chicken of the woods • Dryad's saddle • Giant puffball • Sheathed woodtuft • Poplar fieldcap • Shaggy mane 
• Leave fallen leaves on beds. • Collect leaves on grass and paths to make leaf mold.	• Black-staining polypore • Blewits • Honey fungus • Hen of the woods 

FAQS

Can I eat it? Some garden fungi are edible, but leave fruiting bodies for wildlife if you are uncertain of their identity—never munch on a hunch.

Can I touch it? Absolutely! Fungi don't sting or scratch as some plants do. Poisonous fungi must be eaten to have any ill effects. Only by handling fruiting bodies will you be able to fully appreciate all their identifying features. Just wash hands afterward, as with any gardening.

Can fungi be identified from photos? Fruiting bodies in poor-quality photos are usually unrecognizable. To successfully obtain expert help, provide a set of well-lit, close-up photographs showing all angles, the spore color, and a cross section with notes on sensory characteristics and context.

Someone in my care has consumed fruiting bodies that I don't recognize; what should I do? Seek medical help immediately. Take samples if there are more of the same type of fruiting body available. For nonemergency help about fungal poisons, contact the Poison Control Center at 1-800-222-1222.

Is it safe to breathe in fungal spores? Normal air contains lots of spores, which usually cause no problems in healthy adults. Fungal infections or allergies can result from prolonged exposure to spores, especially in adults with compromised immunity, elderly people, or young children. Certain fungi are especially harmful to vulnerable people, such as the compost heap mold (*Aspergillus fumigatus*) and black mold (*Stachybotrys chartarum*).

Why are there fruiting bodies in my plant pot/lawn/compost? Healthy compost and soil contains fungal networks (mycelia) that recycle dead organic matter, using some to feed themselves and releasing the rest, which improves the availability of nutrients for plants growing there. Fruiting bodies appear so the fungi can reproduce by spreading its spores. They require a lot of water so may indicate that your pot, lawn, or heap is too wet.

Can I stop problematic fruiting bodies from coming back? Fungi will fruit until they run out of food or are outcompeted by other fungi. Picking fruiting bodies will not remove the mycelium embedded within the substrate but might help if your problem concerns preventing accidental ingestion. To slow or deter a fungus, you need to alter the substrate either by aerating, mechanically disturbing, drying it, or, for timber, potentially retreating it.

What should I do with fruiting bodies that I need to remove? Fruiting bodies can be picked off and placed elsewhere, for example, in the branches of bushes or trees, so their spores will be spread by the wind. You can also compost them if you are happy that their mycelium may spread into the compost heap.

My tree has fungi growing on the bark, what should I do? Most fungi on trees are rotting dead sections of wood and are not harming the tree, so you can enjoy seeing their fruiting bodies appear. Hire a qualified arborist to monitor and manage aging trees with fungi in case weak spots are forming, which could lead to limbs or trunks breaking in high winds. You can tell if a fungus is harming the living sapwood when the bark is deformed or weeping and the canopy looks sparse. Cutting off infected branches could prevent infection spreading to the rest of the tree. If the trunk is infected, removing the tree could prevent infection spreading.

There is a fungus causing disease on my plants' leaves; what should I do? Only if you have spotted the infection at the very start of the outbreak should you try to prune off the infected leaves. Avoid overhead watering, which will encourage the infection to spread. Tolerate advanced infections for the season and work in the off-season to reduce infection next year by cleaning up fallen infected leaves, pruning out infected stems, improving airflow around the plant, and adding a thick layer of mulch.

How can I tell if I have the "bad" honey fungus? Consider how healthy a plant was before it died. Stressed, young, or old plants could have been taken advantage of by the weaker pathogen (*Armillaria gallica*), whereas healthy, mature plants that decline quickly, or lots of deaths in a year or two, suggest infection was by the true pathogenic species (*A. mellea*).

My tree/shrub with honey fungus root rot has died, can I chip the top to use in the garden? Yes, honey fungus root rot tends not to climb high up the trunk. Check under the bark for the frontier of the white mycelial fans or the soft wet rot. Anything 6in (15cm) above that should be safe to use.

How do I ensure good hygiene when managing pathogenic fungal infections? Clean tools, boots, and gloves with disinfectant after contacting diseased material. Bag up diseased material where it is pruned to carry it away. Hot composting may be able to kill leaf pathogens, but cool compost probably will not. Alternatively, burn infected leaves or send them for green waste collection. Dispose of infected wood by burning.

Where can I submit records of wild fungi that I have found and identified? You can make an account on a range of websites and submit records of spontaneously fruiting fungi (not cultivation projects). Some options to upload and explore records are inaturalist.org, mycoportal.org, and you can explore records on gbif.org.

How can I find local fungal spawn and materials for home-growing projects? Refer to fungi.com, fieldforest.net, northspore.com, or find suppliers in your area and email them to provide information on the provenance of the strains in their collection.

BIBLIOGRAPHY

CHAPTER 1

Crous, P. W., Rossman, A. Y., Aime, M. C., Allen, W. C., Burgess, T., Groenewald, J. Z., and Castlebury, L. A., 2021. Names of Phytopathogenic Fungi: A Practical Guide. *Phytopathology*, 111(9), pp.1500–1508. doi.org/10.1094/PHYTO-11-20-0512-PER

Hyde, K., 2024. The 2024 Outline of Fungi and fungus-like taxa. *Mycosphere*, 15(1), pp.5146–6239. doi.org/10.5943/mycosphere/15/1/25

Boddy, L., Hynes, J., Bebber, D. P. and Fricker, M. D., 2009. Saprotrophic cord systems: dispersal mechanisms in space and time. *Mycoscience*, 50(1), pp.9–19. doi.org/10.1007/S10267-008-0450-4

Fruiting bodies

O'Reilly, P., 2022. *Fascinated by Fungi: exploring the history, mystery, facts and fiction of the underworld kingdom of mushrooms.* Machynlleth, Powys: Coch-y-Bonddu Books.

Fröhlich-Nowoisky, J., Pickersgill, D. A., Després, V. R., and Pöschl, U., 2009. High diversity of fungi in air particulate matter. *Proceedings of the National Academy of Sciences*, 106(31), pp.12814–12819. doi.org/10.1073/pnas.0811003106

Moore, D., 1996. Graviresponses in fungi. *Advances in space research: the official journal of the Committee on Space Research (COSPAR)*, 17(6–7), pp.73–82. doi.org/10.1016/0273-1177(95)00614-k

RHS Honey fungus: identifying mushrooms www.rhs.org.uk/disease/honey-fungus-identifying-mushrooms

Identification

Fatto, R., Kibby, G., and Evans, S., 2000. Cross-off sheets for easy recording of fungi. *Field Mycology*, 1(4), pp.126–127. doi.org/10.1016/S1468-1641(10)60065-5

Nichol, P., 2017. *An initial guide to the identification of mushrooms and toadstools*. Fourth edition. ed. East Midlands.

Kibby, G., 2020–2023. *Mushrooms and toadstools of Britain & Europe*. Volumes 1–4. Great Britain: Geoffrey Kibby.

Laessøe, T. and Petersen, J. H., 2019. *Fungi of temperate Europe*. Princeton Oxford: Princeton University Press.

Phillips, R., Reid, D. A., Rayner, R., Kibby, G., Henrici, A., and Bryan, J., 2006. *Mushrooms: a comprehensive guide with over 1250 detailed photographs of mushrooms and other fungi*. London: Macmillan.

Storey, M., 2016. Mycological Microscopy part 1: choosing your equipment. *Field Mycology*, 17(4), pp.114–123. doi.org/10.1016/j.fldmyc.2016.10.004

First Nature Fungi Index: www.first-nature.com/fungi/~id-guide.php

Moss, M.O., 2000. Setting up the microscope part 1. *Field Mycology*, 1(4), pp.128–130. doi.org/10.1016/S1468-1641(10)60066-7

Lecomte, M., Baar, D., Fortin, G., and Pirlot, J. M., 2024. *Microscopy & Fungi: = Mycology and Microscopy*. 1st English edition ed. AMBF (Association des Mycologues Francophones de Belgique).

Field mycologists map fungi with DNA barcoding. bento.bio/blog/2020/07/24/dna-enabling-uk-field-mycologists-to-discover-new-species-and-dna-barcode-fungal-biodiversity

Fungi in ecosystems

Konuma, R., Umezawa, K., Mizukoshi, A., Kawarada, K., and Yoshida, M., 2015. Analysis of microbial volatile organic compounds produced by wood-decay fungi. *Biotechnology Letters*, 37(9), pp.1845–1852. doi.org/10.1007/s10529-015-1870-9

Niego, A. G. T., Rapior, S., Thongklang, N., Raspé, O., Hyde, K. D., and Mortimer, P., 2023. Reviewing the contributions of macrofungi to forest ecosystem processes and services. *Fungal Biology Reviews*, 44, p.100294. doi.org/10.1016/j.fbr.2022.11.002

Crowther, T. W., Boddy, L., and Hefin Jones, T., 2012. Functional and ecological consequences of saprotrophic fungus–grazer interactions. *The ISME Journal*, 6(11), pp.1992–2001. doi.org/10.1038/ismej.2012.53

CHAPTER 2

Habitat

Omomowo, I. O., Amao, J. A., Abubakar, A., Ogundola, A. F., Ezediuno, L. O., and Bamigboye, C. O., 2023. A review on the trends of endophytic fungi bioactivities. *Scientific African*, 20, p.e01594. doi.org/10.1016/j.sciaf.2023.e01594

Ainsworth, A., 2005. 6. Fungal species of conservation concern (SoCC): taxonomic relationships. *BAP fungi handbook*. English Nature Research Reports

IUCN Red List of threatened species: www.iucnredlist.org/en

Mueller, G. M., Cunha, K. M., May, T. W., Allen, J. L., Westrip, J. R. S., Canteiro, C., Costa-Rezende, D. H., Drechsler-Santos, E. R., Vasco-Palacios, A. M., Ainsworth, A. M., Alves-Silva, G., Bungartz, F., Chandler, A., Gonçalves, S. C., Krisai-Greilhuber, I., Iršėnaitė, R., Jordal, J. B., Kosmann, T., Lendemer,

J., McMullin, R. T., Mešić, A., Motato-Vásquez, V., Ohmura, Y., Næsborg, R. R., Perini, C., Saar, I., Simijaca, D., Yahr, R., and Dahlberg, A., 2022. What Do the First 597 Global Fungal Red List Assessments Tell Us about the Threat Status of Fungi? *Diversity*, 14(9), p.736. doi.org/10.3390/d14090736

Haelewaters, D., Quandt, C. A., Bartrop, L., Cazabonne, J., Crockatt, M. E., Cunha, S. P., De Lange, R., Dominici, L., Douglas, B., Drechsler Santos, E. R., Heilmann Clausen, J., Irga, P. J., Jakob, S., Lofgren, L., Martin, T. E., Muchane, M. N., Stallman, J. K., Verbeken, A., Walker, A. K., and Gonçalves, S. C., 2024. The power of citizen science to advance fungal conservation. *Conservation Letters*, 17(3), p.e13013. doi.org/10.1111/conl.13013

Bruce, A. L., 2018. *Population genomic insights into the establishment of non-native golden oyster mushrooms (Pleurotus citrinopileatus) in the United States*. [Thesis] minds.wisconsin.edu/handle/1793/79004

Foraging

Dann, G., 2016. *Edible Mushrooms: A forager's guide to the wild fungi of Britain and Europe*. Totnes: UIT Cambridge Ltd.

Woodchip

Linda Chalker-Scott (compiled by). Literature on Landscape Use of Wood Chips. puyallup.wsu.edu/lcs/reference-wood-chips

Heartwood

Humphries, D. and Wright, C., 2021. *Fungi on trees: a photographic reference*. Standish, Stonehouse, Gloucestershire: Arboricultural Association.

Boddy, L., 2021. *Fungi and trees: their complex relationships*. Gloucestershire: Arboricultural Association.

RHS heartwood fungi: www.rhs.org.uk/biodiversity/heartwood-fungi

Overall, A., 2016. Southern Bracket or Artist's Conk? *Field Mycology*, 17(4), pp.124–128. doi.org/10.1016/j.fldmyc.2016.10.005

Dead trees

Green, T., 2000. A rare fungus and rare trees. *Field Mycology*, 1(4), pp.133–134. doi.org/10.1016/S1468-1641(10)60070-9

Purahong, W., Wubet, T., Krüger, D., and Buscot, F., 2018. Molecular evidence strongly supports deadwood-inhabiting fungi exhibiting unexpected tree species preferences in temperate forests. *The ISME Journal*, 12(1), pp.289–295. doi.org/10.1038/ismej.2017.177

Buglife, 2022. Back from the Brink: Managing dead and decaying wood habitats. cdn.buglife.org.uk/2022/01/BFTB-Advice-Sheet-Managing-Dead-and-Decaying-Wood.FINAL_.pdf

Fallen wood

RHS Saprotrophic fungi: www.rhs.org.uk/biodiversity/saprotrophic-fungi

Moose, R. A., Schigel, D., Kirby, L. J., and Shumskaya, M., 2019. Dead wood fungi in North America: an insight into research and conservation potential. *Nature Conservation*, 32, pp.1–17. doi.org/10.3897/natureconservation.32.30875

Leaf litter

Fanin, N., Lin, D., Freschet, G. T., Keiser, A. D., Augusto, L., Wardle, D. A., and Veen, G. F. (Ciska), 2021. Home-field advantage of litter decomposition: from the phyllosphere to the soil. *New Phytologist*, 231(4), pp.1353–1358. doi.org/10.1111/nph.17475

Pugnaire, F. I., Aares, K. H., Alifriqui, M., Bråthen, K. A., Kindler, C., Schöb, C., and Manrique, E., 2023. Home-field advantage effects in litter decomposition is largely linked to litter quality. *Soil Biology and Biochemistry*, 184, p.109069. doi.org/10.1016/j.soilbio.2023.109069

Grass and lawns

Andrew P. Detheridge and Gareth W. Griffith, 2021. *Standards, methodology and protocols for sampling and identification of grassland fungus species: Using eDNA from soil samples.* Natural England commissioned report. UK: Natural England.

Wood, E. and Dunkelman, J., 2017. *Grassland fungi: a field guide*. Monmouth: Monmouthshire Meadows Group.

Schenk-Jaeger, K. M., Hofer-Lentner, K. E., Plenert, B., Eckart, D., Haberl, B., Schulze, G., Borchert-Avalone, J., Stedtler, U., and Pfab, R., 2017. No clinically relevant effects in children after accidental ingestion of Panaeolina foenisecii (lawn mower's mushroom). *Clinical Toxicology (Philadelphia, Pa.)*, 55(3), pp.217–220. doi.org/10.1080/15563650.2016.1271129

Soil

Ohio State University—Role of Soil Fungus. ohioline.osu.edu/factsheet/anr-37

Irving, T. B., Alptekin, B., Kleven, B., and Ané, J., 2021. A critical review of 25 years of glomalin research: a better mechanical understanding and robust quantification techniques are required. *New Phytologist*, 232(4), pp.1572–1581. doi.org/10.1111/nph.17713

Schlatter, D., Kinkel, L., Thomashow, L., Weller, D., and Paulitz, T., 2017. Disease Suppressive Soils: New Insights from the Soil Microbiome. *Phytopathology®*, 107(11), pp.1284–1297. doi.org/10.1094/PHYTO-03-17-0111-RVW

Spooner, B., 2000. The larger cup fungi in Britain—part 1. *Field Mycology*, 1(4), pp.137–139. doi.org/10.1016/S1468-1641(10)60072-2

Mycorrhizae

RHS mycorrhizal fungi: www.rhs.org.uk/biodiversity/mycorrhizal-fungi

Thirkell, T. J., Charters, M. D., Elliott, A. J., Sait, S. M., and Field, K. J., 2017. Are mycorrhizal fungi our sustainable saviours? Considerations for achieving food security. *Journal of Ecology*, 105(4), pp.921–929. doi.org/10.1111/1365-2745.12788

Akyol, T. Y., Niwa, R., Hirakawa, H., Maruyama, H., Sato, T., Suzuki, T., Fukunaga, A., Sato, T., Yoshida, S., Tawaraya, K., Saito, M., Ezawa, T., and Sato, S., 2019. Impact of Introduction of Arbuscular Mycorrhizal Fungi on the Root Microbial Community in Agricultural Fields. *Microbes and Environments*, 34(1), pp.23–32. doi.org/10.1264/jsme2.ME18109

Miransari, M., 2011. Interactions between arbuscular mycorrhizal fungi and soil bacteria. *Applied Microbiology and Biotechnology*, 89(4), pp.917–930. doi.org/10.1007/s00253-010-3004-6

Jargeat, P., Chaumeton, J. P., Navaud, O., Vizzini, A., and Gryta, H., 2014. The *Paxillus involutus* (*Boletales*, *Paxillaceae*) complex in Europe: Genetic diversity and morphological description of the new species *Paxillus cuprinus*, typification of *P. involutus* s.s., and synthesis of species boundaries. *Fungal Biology*, 118(1), pp.12–31. doi.org/10.1016/j.funbio.2013.10.008

Pathogens

Greenwood, P. and Halstead, A., 2018. *Pests & Diseases*. New edition. ed. London: Dorling Kindersley Limited in association with the Royal Horticultural Society.

Buczacki, S., Harris, K., and Hargreaves, B., 2010. *Pests, Diseases and Disorders of Garden Plants*. S.l.: HarperCollins Publishers. (Out of print but available as ebook.)

RHS preventing pest and disease problems: www.rhs.org.uk/prevention-protection/preventing-pest-and-disease-problems

RHS pear rust: www.rhs.org.uk/disease/pear-rust

RHS powdery mildews: www.rhs.org.uk/disease/powdery-mildews

RHS honey fungus: www.rhs.org.uk/disease/honey-fungus

RHS honey fungus plant list: www.rhs.org.uk/advice/pdfs/honey-fungus-host-list.pdf www.rhs.org.uk/disease/honey-fungus-identifying-mushrooms

RHS yucca leaf spot: www.rhs.org.uk/disease/yucca-leaf-spot

RHS silver leaf: www.rhs.org.uk/disease/silver-leaf

NIAB symptoms and recognition (Silver leaf): www.niab.com/symptoms-and-recognition-silver-leaf

Percival, G., Silver Leaf Identification, Biology & Management. [Bartlett Tree Experts Research Laboratory Technical Report] p.2. www.bartlett.com/resources/silver-leaf.pdf

Arboriculture blog: *Fungus spotlight:* Phellinus pomaceus *(cushion bracket).* arboriculture.wordpress.com/2016/03/12/fungus-spotlight-phellinus-pomaceus-cushion-bracket

CHAPTER 3

Encouraging healthy soils

AHDB What soil organic matter is and what it does. ahdb.org.uk/knowledge-library/what-soil-organic-matter-is-and-what-it-does

Koziol, L., McKenna, T. P., and Bever, J. D., 2024. Meta-analysis reveals globally sourced commercial mycorrhizal inoculants fall short. *New Phytologist*, [online] p.nph.20278. doi.org/10.1111/nph.20278

Müller, A., Ngwene, B., Peiter, E., and George, E., 2017. Quantity and distribution of arbuscular mycorrhizal fungal storage organs within dead roots. *Mycorrhiza,* 27(3), pp.201–210. doi.org/10.1007/s00572-016-0741-0

Creating habitats

RHS woody waste: using as a mulch www.rhs.org.uk/soil-composts-mulches/woody-waste-using-as-mulch

RHS leaf mold: www.rhs.org.uk/soil-composts-mulches/leaf-mould

RHS composting: www.rhs.org.uk/soil-composts-mulches/composting

Compost: www.charlesdowding.co.uk/resources/compost

Compost microorganisms: compost.css.cornell.edu/microorg.html

Zhu, L., Wang, X., Liu, L., Le, B., Tan, C., Dong, C., Yao, X., and Hu, B., 2024. Fungi play a crucial role in sustaining microbial networks and accelerating organic matter mineralization and humification during thermophilic phase of composting. *Environmental Research*, 254, p.119155. doi.org/10.1016/j.envres.2024.119155

Edibles and outdoor growing

Boddy, L., Crockatt, M. E., and Ainsworth, A. M., 2011. Ecology of *Hericium cirrhatum*, *H. coralloides* and *H. erinaceus* in the UK. *Fungal Ecology*, [online] 4(2), pp.163–173. doi.org/10.1016/j.funeco.2010.10.001

Cultivation projects
RHS grow your own mushrooms outdoors: rhs.org.uk/growmushroomsoutdoors

Fat Fox Mushrooms: growing kit instructions: www.fatfoxmushrooms.com/instructions

Mushroom species to tree species info table: www.gourmetmushrooms.co.uk/mushroom-species-to-tree-species-info-table

Propagation
Mycostart: mycologyst.art/mushroom-cultivation/cultivation-equipment/still-air-box-sab

CHAPTER 4
Gange, A. C., Gange, E. G., Sparks, T. H., and Boddy, L., 2007. Rapid and Recent Changes in Fungal Fruiting Patterns. *Science*, 316(5821), p.71. doi.org/10.1126/science.1137489

Herman, K. C. and Bleichrodt, R., 2022. Go with the flow: mechanisms driving water transport during vegetative growth and fruiting. *Fungal Biology Reviews*, 41, pp.10–23. doi.org/10.1016/j.fbr.2021.10.002

Voříšková, J., Brabcová, V., Cajthaml, T., and Baldrian, P., 2014. Seasonal dynamics of fungal communities in a temperate oak forest soil. *New Phytologist*, 201(1), pp.269–278. doi.org/10.1111/nph.12481

Hofmann, D., Preuss, G., and Mätzler, C., 2015. Evidence for biological shaping of hair ice. *Biogeosciences*, 12(14), pp.4261–4273. doi.org/10.5194/bg-12-4261-2015

Smith, K. T., 2019. A few winter fungi. *Mainely Mushrooms*, 35(1), pp.9–12 www.fs.usda.gov/nrs/pubs/jrnl/2019/nrs_2019_smith-k_001.pdf

Useful resources

Identification
Mycological information site useful for identification: mycobank.org

Index of Fungi: www.cabi.org/publishing-products/index-of-fungi/

Fungal records
Scientific data information facility: www.gbif.org

Record your findings and share them with others: www.iNaturalist.org

Global Biodiversity Information Facility: www.gbif.org

IUCN Red List of threatened species: www.iucnredlist.org/en

Pathogen
Greenwood, P. and Halstead, A., 2018. *Pests & Diseases*. New edition. ed. London: Dorling Kindersley Limited in association with the Royal Horticultural Society.

Cultivation projects
Grow your own mushrooms outdoors: https://northspore.com/pages/mushroom-garden?srsltid=AfmBOop3gcDVCPnpnlxDZdwPfybCM1xiIWDTKDkPs-bhrycNK8aKY6gp

Glossary

Endophyte
Fungus living inside living plant tissues

Fruiting body
Structure made by the fungus to produce and shed spores

Hyphae
Microscopic, threadlike fungal cells

Mycelium
An interconnected network of hyphae (how fungi mainly live)

Mycorrhiza (plural mycorrhizae)
Fungus living in partnership with living plant roots

Plant pathogenic fungus
Fungus living in and causing harm to a living plant

Recycler fungus
Fungus that breaks down and feeds on dead material, known scientifically as a saprotroph

Rhizomorph
Visible, thick cords made of bundles of hyphae and protective coat

Spore
Reproductive cell that initiates the growth of a new fungus

Spawn
Fungal mycelium growing on a food source (substrate) used to propagate the fungus

Substrate
Dead plant material to feed and grow recycler fungi on

INDEX

Note: page numbers in **bold** refer to information contained in captions.

About the author

Dr. Jassy Drakulic is a plant pathologist and mycologist, promoting understanding and appreciation for fungal biodiversity in gardens. She leads the honey fungus research program at the RHS, investigating its biology and ecology in UK gardens, and developing sustainable ways for gardeners to manage its root rot. She also supports the RHS Gardening Advice Service, identifying and explaining the impacts of fungi to domestic gardeners and providing management advice about plant diseases.

Author's acknowledgments

Thanks to Helen Griffin, Lucy Philpott, Amy Child, Nicola Hodgson, Glenda Fisher, and Rosie Holman for your diligence and artistry while producing this book.

I am deeply grateful to the many mycologists who have supported me, especially Geoffrey Kibby, Lorin von Longo-Liebenstein, Fay Newbery, Rich Wright, and Lynne Boddy whose inputs have directly shaped this book.

Warm thanks to my friends, family members, colleagues, and collaborators for their belief and encouragement—especially the "Armi Army" and those growing native fungi outdoors. To my husband, Sabri, and son, Ralph, thank you for your love, care, and forgiveness for all the times I have left decaying fruiting bodies in the fridge.

Publisher's acknowledgments

DK would like to thank Vagisha Pushp for the picture credits, Katie Hewett for proofreading, Linda Chalker-Scott for consulting on the US edition, and Lisa Footitt for indexing.

Picture credits

The publisher would like to thank the following for their kind permission to reproduce their photographs:

(Key: a-above; b-below/bottom; c-centre; f-far; l-left; r-right; t-top)

Adobe Stock: ecOde 10-11, 26-27, 90-91, 120-121; **Alamy Stock Photo:** All Canada Photos / Tim Zurowski 21cl, Sally Anderson 66bl, Arterra Picture Library / Clement Philippe 49tl, blickwinkel / F. Hecker 127tl, Chris Hellier 67tr, Juniors Bildarchiv GmbH / Schulz, H. / juniors@wildlife 96, Henri Koskinen 82br, Justin Long 13tl, Roel Meijer 71crb, Nature Picture Library / Andy Sands 77crb, piemags / nature 89bl, Christian Weinkötz 34br; **Dreamstime.com:** Jm73 123br; naturepl.com: Andy Sands 61tl; **RHS:** Liz Beal 84br, Samuel Booth 129cla, Jassy Drakulic 12bl, 12br, 21tl, 21tr, 21bl, 24bl, 31, 41tr, 42bc, 43tr, 48br, 54br, 55tr, 75br, 84bl, 86bl, 87tr, 88br, 93, 99, 101tr, 101cla, 105tr, 105br, 107, 111, 119tr, 119br, 122-123bc, 123tl, 125tl, 125cla, 125bl, 126-127bc, 127tr, 127cra, 129tl, 129tr, 131tl, 131clb, 131bl, Simon Garbutt 125tr, Neil Hepworth 95b, Katy Hubbuck 123cr, Tim Sandall 85tl, 95tl, 95cra, 101tl, 103br, Carol Sheppard 129bl, Staff Member 85tr; **Shutterstock.com:** Tintila Corina 76crb

DK
Editorial Director Ruth O'Rourke
Project Editor Lucy Philpott
US Senior Editor Jennette ElNaggar
Senior Designer Glenda Fisher
Senior Production Editor Tony Phipps
Senior Production Controller Samantha Cross
Jacket Designer Glenda Fisher
Jacket and Sales Material Coordinator Emily Cannings
Art Director Maxine Pedliham
Publishing Director Stephanie Jackson

Editorial Nicola Hodgson
Design Amy Child
Illustration Rosie Holman, Dan Crisp
Jacket illustration Rosie Holman

ROYAL HORTICULTURAL SOCIETY
Consultants Simon Maughan, Mike Grant, Alistair Griffiths
Books Publisher Helen Griffin
Head of Editorial Tom Howard

First American Edition, 2025
Published in the United States by DK Publishing,
a division of Penguin Random House LLC
1745 Broadway, 20th Floor, New York, NY 10019

25 26 27 28 29 10 9 8 7 6 5 4 3 2 1
001-355662-Oct/2025

Published in Great Britain by Dorling Kindersley Limited

ISBN 979-8-2171-3762-6

Printed and bound in China

www.dk.com

This book was made with Forest Stewardship Council™ certified paper–one small step in DK's commitment to a sustainable future.
For more information go to www.dk.com/our-green-pledge